EVOCATING THE GODS

Evocating the Gods

DIVINE EVOCATION
IN THE
GRÆCO-EGYPTIAN MAGICAL PAPYRI

Christopher A. Plaisance

Published by Avalonia
www.avaloniabooks.co.uk

PUBLISHED BY AVALONIA
BM AVALONIA, LONDON, WC1N 3XX, ENGLAND, UK
WWW.AVALONIABOOKS.CO.UK

EVOCATING THE GODS: DIVINE EVOCATION IN THE
GRÆCO-EGYPTIAN MAGICAL PAPYRI
COPYRIGHT © CHRISTOPHER A. PLAISANCE, 2019
ALL RIGHTS RESERVED.

FIRST PUBLISHED BY AVALONIA, APRIL 2020
ISBN 978-1-910191-18-7

TYPESET AND DESIGNED BY CHRISTOPHER A. PLAISANCE
COVER IMAGE COPYRIGHT © 2019 BY MITCHELL NOLTE

ILLUSTRATIONS AND PHOTOGRAPHS THROUGHOUT THIS VOLUME © AS CREDITED, OTHERWISE © THE AUTHOR.

EVERY EFFORT HAS BEEN MADE TO CREDIT MATERIAL AND TO OBTAIN PERMISSION FROM THE COPYRIGHT HOLDERS FOR THE USE OF THEIR WORK. IF YOU NOTICE ANY ERROR OR OMISSION PLEASE NOTIFY THE PUBLISHER SO THAT CORRECTIONS CAN BE INCORPORATED INTO FUTURE EDITIONS OF THIS WORK.

THE INFORMATION PROVIDED IN THIS BOOK HOPES TO INSPIRE AND INFORM. THE AUTHOR AND PUBLISHER ASSUME NO RESPONSIBILITY FOR THE EFFECTS, OR LACK THEREOF, OBTAINED FROM THE PRACTICES DESCRIBED IN THIS BOOK.

THIS BOOK IS SOLD SUBJECT TO THE CONDITION THAT NO PART OF IT MAY BE REPRODUCED OR UTILIZED IN ANY FORM OR BY ANY MEANS, ELECTRONIC OR MECHANICAL, INCLUDING PHOTOCOPYING, MICROFILM, RECORDING, OR BY ANY INFORMATION STORAGE AND RETRIEVAL SYSTEM, OR USED IN ANOTHER BOOK, WITHOUT WRITTEN PERMISSION FROM THE AUTHOR, WITH THE EXCEPTION OF BRIEF QUOTATIONS IN REVIEWS OR ARTICLES WHERE APPROPRIATE CREDIT IS GIVEN TO THE COPYRIGHT HOLDER.

BRITISH LIBRARY CATALOGUING IN PUBLICATION DATA. A CATALOGUE RECORD FOR THIS BOOK IS AVAILABLE FROM THE BRITISH LIBRARY

Contents

List of Figures   v

Abbreviations   vii

Acknowledgements   ix

1 Introduction   1
  1.1 Introducing Θεαγωγία 1
  1.2 Methodology 3
      1.2.1 Methodological Challenges 3
      1.2.2 Essentialism in the Social Sciences 4
      1.2.3 Linguisticism and Philology 5
  1.3 Terms and Definitions 9
      1.3.1 Defining Θεαγωγία 9
      1.3.2 Μαγεία and Γοητεία 12
      1.3.3 Θεουργία 15
          1.3.3.1 Origins of Θεουργία 15
          1.3.3.2 Σύστασις 16
          1.3.3.3 Τελεστική 17
          1.3.3.4 Ἀναγωγή 19
      1.3.4 "Magical" Disjunctions 20

2 Spells of Binding and Constraint   25
  2.1 Κατάδεσμοι and *Defixiones* 25
      2.1.1 Curse Tablets in the Graeco-Roman World 25
      2.1.2 Curse Tablet Materials 27
      2.1.3 Creators of the Curse Tablets 30
  2.2 Theory and Practice 31
      2.2.1 Functional Classification 31

	2.2.2	Classification by *Modus Operandi*	32
		2.2.2.1 Unmediated Operations	32
		2.2.2.2 Supernatural Mediation	33
		2.2.2.3 Wish Formulae and *Similia Similibus*	34
2.3	Gods, Daemons, and Ghosts		35
	2.3.1	Theology of the Curse Tablets	35
	2.3.2	Daemonic Intermediaries	36
		2.3.2.1 Origins in the Epic Period	36
		2.3.2.2 Platonic Transformations	37
		2.3.2.3 Hecate, Daemons, and the Dead	38
		2.3.2.4 Intermediary Nexus	40
	2.3.3	Case Study (*PGM* XV)	41
		2.3.3.1 Ritual Mechanics	41
		2.3.3.2 Connections to Θεαγωγία	42

3 Erotic Enchantments 43

- 3.1 Origins of Ἀγωγή . . . 43
  - 3.1.1 Foundational Classifications . . . 43
  - 3.1.2 Early Examples . . . 44
    - 3.1.2.1 Sappho . . . 44
    - 3.1.2.2 Pindar . . . 45
  - 3.1.3 Connections to Bridal Theft Traditions . . . 46
    - 3.1.3.1 Mythological Roots . . . 46
    - 3.1.3.2 Historical Traditions . . . 47
    - 3.1.3.3 Erotic Spells and Bridal Theft . . . 47
- 3.2 Ἀγωγαί and Κατάδεσμοι . . . 49
  - 3.2.1 Connective Matrix . . . 49
  - 3.2.2 Case Study A (The Sword of Dardanos) . . . 50
  - 3.2.3 Case Study B (Φιλτροκατάδεσμος) . . . 51
    - 3.2.3.1 Etymological Questions . . . 51
    - 3.2.3.2 Physical and Emotional Bondage . . . 52
    - 3.2.3.3 Paired Effigies . . . 53
- 3.3 Ἀνάγκη and Spells of Compulsion . . . 55
  - 3.3.1 Compulsion and Θεαγωγία . . . 55
  - 3.3.2 Ἀνάγκη in the *PGM* . . . 56
  - 3.3.3 Case Study (*PGM* IV.2891–2942) . . . 57
    - 3.3.3.1 Structure of the Spell . . . 57
    - 3.3.3.2 Divine Compulsion . . . 58

CONTENTS   iii

      3.3.3.3 The Importance of Ὁρκίζω 58

4 **Psychagogy and Necromancy**   **61**
 4.1 From Ἔρως to Θάνατος 61
   4.1.1 Compelling the Dead 61
   4.1.2 Case Studies 62
      4.1.2.1 PGM IV.1390–1495 62
      4.1.2.2 PGM IV.2708–84 63
   4.1.3 Ritual Analysis 65
 4.2 Corpse Animation and Soul Evocation 66
   4.2.1 King Pitys the Necromancer 66
   4.2.2 Two of Pitys' Spells 67
      4.2.2.1 PGM IV.2140–44 67
      4.2.2.2 PGM IV.1928–2125 68
 4.3 An Exegesis of PGM IV.2006–2125 70
   4.3.1 Pitys' Evocation 70
   4.3.2 A Coactive Operation 71
   4.3.3 The Necro-Daemon 72
   4.3.4 Teleology 73
   4.3.5 Necromantic Dream Divination 74
   4.3.6 Ψυχαγωγία, Θεαγωγία, and Ἀγωγή 75

5 **Evocating the Gods**   **77**
 5.1 Θεαγωγία and the Ph-ntr Spells of the PDM . . . 77
   5.1.1 Linguistic Roots of Ph-ntr 77
   5.1.2 Egyptian Magical Theory 78
   5.1.3 Spells in the Demotic Corpus 80
   5.1.4 Bilingual Graeco-Egyptian Spells 81
 5.2 An Exegesis of PGM IV.930–1114 82
   5.2.1 The Spell's Title 82
   5.2.2 Section I 83
      5.2.2.1 Defining Σύστασις 83
      5.2.2.2 An Αὐτοψία Hymn 85
      5.2.2.3 Lychnomancy 86
   5.2.3 Section II 86
   5.2.4 Section III 87
   5.2.5 Section IV 89
   5.2.6 Section V 89
   5.2.7 Sections VI–VIII 90

		5.2.8	Sections IX–XII	91
	5.3	Θεαγωγία in Later Platonism		92
		5.3.1	Porphyry	92
		5.3.2	Iamblichus	93
			5.3.2.1 Θεαγωγία Contra Θεουργία	93
			5.3.2.2 Θεαγωγία and Impiety	94
			5.3.2.3 Evocation and the Luminous Vehicle	95
		5.3.3	Gregory of Nazianzus	96
		5.3.4	Basil of Seleucia	96
		5.3.5	Proclus	97
		5.3.6	Michael Psellus	97
		5.3.7	Gregory Palamas	98

6 Conclusion   **99**

Bibliography   **103**

Index Locorum   **122**

Index Nominum   **129**

Index Rerum   **132**

Index Verborum Demoticorum   **137**

Index Verborum Graecorum   **138**

Index Verborum Latinorum   **145**

List of Figures

1.1 A statue of a leontocephaline Mithraic deity, similar to Helios Mithras Aion as described in *PGM* IV.475–829, from the Vatican Museum's collection. Photo by Vassil, 2017. 21

2.1 A Roman marble copy of a Hellenistic original statue depicting Hecate's triple-formed representation, from the Museo Chiaramonti's collection (Inv. 1922). Photo by Jastrow, 2006. 39

3.1 The effigy found paired with the papyrus on which *PGM* IV.296–466 is attested, currently in the Louvre Museum's collection (E 27145b). Photo by Marie-Lan Nguyen, 2014. 54

4.1 The so-called "Burney Relief" (c. 1800–1750 BC), depicting a Babylonian underworld goddess, likely Ereshkigal. Photo by Aiwok, 2011. 64

5.1 A statue in cast bronze of Horus, as Harpocrates, seated on a lotus (664–322 BC), from the Walters Art Museum collection (54.419). Photo by the Walters Art Museum, 2012. 84

Abbreviations

CDD *The Demotic Dictionary of the Oriental Insitute of the University of Chicago*, ed. by Janet H. Johnson (Chicago: The Oriental Institute of the University of Chicago, 2002)

DT *Defixionum tabellae*, ed. by Augustus Audollent (Paris: Fontemoing, 1904)

DTA *Defixionum tabellae Atticae*, ed. by Richard Wünsch, Corpus inscriptionum Atticarum (Berlin: Georgium Reimerum, 1897)

GMPT *The Greek Magical Papyri in Translation, Including the Demotic Spells*, ed. by Hans Dieter Betz, trans. by Hans Dieter Betz et al. (Chicago: The University of Chicago Press, 1986)

LMPG *Lexico de magia y religión en los papiros mágicos griegos*, ed. by L. Muñoz Delgado and J. Ródriguez Somolinos, Diccionario Griego-Español 5 (Madrid: CSIC, 2001)

LSJ *A Greek-English Lexicon*, ed. by Henry Georgy Liddell and Robert Scott, rev. by Henry Stuart Jones and Roderick McKenzie (Oxford: Clarendon Press, 1996)

PDM *Papyri Demoticae magicae* (as cited in *GMPT*)

PGM *Papyri Graecae magicae: Die Griechischen Zauberpapyri*, 2 vols., ed. and trans. by Karl Preisendanz (Leipzig: Teubner, 1928–1931)

SM *Supplementum magicum*, 2 vols., ed. by Robert Walter Daniel and Franco Maltomini, Papyrologica Coloniensia 16.1–2 (Opladen: Westdeutscher Verlag, 1990–1992)

Acknowledgements

This monograph is based on the thesis written towards the completion of my MA in Western Esotericism with the University of Exeter's Centre for the Study of Esotericism (EXESESO). The initial version was composed under the tutelage of my advisor, Angela Voss, who I thank for supervising this descent in the "Platonic Underworld," and for her careful critique of the early drafts. The monograph's completion would not have been possible if not for the patience and support of my wife, Diana, and our children, Merrick and Juliet. I also owe great debts to several colleagues, who variously reviewed early drafts of this work's chapters, discussed with me its core issues, and aided in translating some of the more difficult passages — most especially Edward P. Butler, Kyle Fraser, Jeffrey S. Kupperman, and Damon Zacharias Lycourinos. And finally, this work could not have been accomplished if not for he who Iamblichus described thusly: "Θεὸς ὁ τῶν λόγων ἡγεμῶν" (*De mysteriis*, I.1.1).

Chapter 1

Introduction

1.1 Introducing Θεαγωγία

Within the extant corpus of Hellenistic literature, there are a small number of attestations of a curious term: θεαγωγία (divine evocation). The use of the terms "evocation" and "invocation" within contemporary discourses on magic exhibit clear technical distinctions — with *invocation* being an activity proper to the supernal genera of beings occupying a higher place than the operator in the divine hierarchy (i.e. gods, angels), and *evocation* referring to activities proper to the infernal classes of beings beneath the operator in the hierarchy (i.e. daemons, spirits). From the perspective of contemporary magical practice, Aleister Crowley provides one of the clearest examples of this discourse:

> To invoke is to call in, just as to evoke is to call forth or out. This is the essential difference between the two branches of Magick. In invocation, the Macrocosm floods the consciousness. In evocation, the Magician, having become the Macrocosm, creates a Microcosm. You invoke a God into the Circle. You evoke a spirit into the Triangle.[1]

In the case that such a fundamental technical distinction exists today, the question is naturally raised: if evocation is something

---
[1] Crowley, *Magick in Theory and Practice*, 147.

an operator does with respect to the inferior classes, what sense did this late antique term make that refers to the evocating the gods? It is precisely this line of reasoning which informs a particularly memorable passage of *De mysteriis*, wherein Iamblichus (AD c. 245–325) castigates those practitioners of θεαγωγία, decrying their art as ἀμαθής (ignorant), ἀλαζονικός (boastful), and ψευδής (false) — in contrast to the γνήσιος (genuine) and ἀληθής (true) θεουργία (divine work) of the philosophers.[2] The picture that emerges from this description is that, for Iamblichus, θεαγωγία stands diametrically opposed to θεουργία, both in terms of efficacy and piety, as an illicit mode of interacting with the gods — a distinction which closely mirrors the contemporary distinction made between the modern technical usages of *evocation* and *invocation* within discourses on magic.

Iamblichus' teacher, Porphyry (AD c. 234–c. 305),[3] as well as the early Byzantine Church fathers such as Gregory of Nazianzus (AD c. 329–389),[4] Basil of Seleucia (fifth century AD),[5] and Gregory Palamas (1296–1359),[6] discuss θεαγωγία in wholly negative terms similar to *De mysteriis*. However, in other sources such as the *Papyri Graecae magicae*,[7] Proclus (AD 412–485),[8] and Michael Psellus (c. 1017–c. 1078),[9] the valuation of θεαγωγία is not nearly as negative. The lengthy spell occurring at *PGM* IV.930–1112, in particular, describes an operation of θεαγωγία in a way that bears a great deal of similarity not only to the

---

[2]Iamblichus, *On the Mysteries*, II.10.92. As it pertains to all subsequent references to Greek texts, while the references given in the footnotes and bibliography correspond to the consulted published edition, the titles given in the monograph's body are consistently the standard Latin translations of the Greek. All translations unless otherwise noted are my own.

[3]Iamblichus quotes Porphyry on θεαγωγία: Ibid., VI.1.241. There is a further fragment given in: Eusebius, *Eusebius Werke viii*, V.10.1–3.

[4]Gregory of Nazianzus, *The Five Theological Orations of Gregory Nazianzus*, I.10.

[5]Basil of Seleucia, *De vita et miraculis sanctae Theclae libri ii*, I.22.10–21.

[6]Palamas, *Epistulae*, III.50.13.

[7]*PGM*, IV.974–75, IV.985–87. For this and all subsequent citations from the *PGM*, the English translation consulted was the *GMPT*. Further related material is to be found in the *SM*.

[8]Proclus' opinion on θεαγωγία is quoted in: Michael Psellus, *Orationes forensis et acta*, I.303–41.

[9]Michael Psellus, *Pselli theologica*, I.27.188–93.

more "religiously" oriented spells of the magical papyri, but also to Iamblichus' own θεουργία. This ambiguity among late antique and medieval Hellenistic authors as to the nature of θεαγωγία casts a pall on any attempts to "fit" the practice into contemporary occultist definitions of evocation and invocation. This being the case, a thorough investigation into the contexts of late antique discourses on θεαγωγία is required to understand the term in a way that is free from presentist hermeneutics that reinterpret its meaning in light of contemporary preconceptions and biases.

At present, the only discussions of θεαγωγία in secondary literature occur in various lexicons, lexigraphic footnotes to primary literature, or as minor points or footnotes in secondary works, which make a broader treatment of the subject necessary at this juncture. The root of my questioning with this monograph is to inquire into the usage of the term θεαγωγία within the *PGM*, to uncover what it meant to those who utilized the term, and to chart the historical connections that exist between it and other related terms and concepts. This research proceeds by demonstrating the connections that exist between θεαγωγία and other technical terms found within the magical papyri, and culminates in an exegesis of *PGM* IV.930–1114. The results of this investigation which I hope to demonstrate are that within the *PGM*, the practice of θεαγωγία appears to be the result of a syncretic confluence between the Egyptian *ph̬-ntr* and the Greek ἀγωγή family of practices. In this way, I believe that such seemingly disparate phenomena can be seen to be tied together, and that θεαγωγία's meaning and historical context can only be understood in relation to these historically related currents of "magic" with which it runs parallel throughout the papyri.

1.2 Methodology

1.2.1 Methodological Challenges

As the subjects with which this monograph deals are frequently categorized under the generalized heading of "magic," a brief excursion into the methodological issues presented by this term is warranted. The difficulties which beset the attempted use of "magic" as an objective classification have led to its description both as a semantic trap,[10] a tainted terminology[11] and a "black hole."[12] In discussing the ways in which scholars have approached the study of "magic," Daniel Ogden identifies two schools of thought, which he terms "essentialist" and "linguistic."[13] The methodology of the essentialist is, according to Ogden, akin to an attempt to uncover the Platonic εἶδος (form) of magic, arriving at a "supreme definition... with a supposed validity across time and place and even across societies and languages."[14] The contrasting linguistic, or philological, methodology focuses not on the construction of "monolithic definitions or concepts" of magic, but rather on the accurate charting of specific "magical" terminologies within their particular cultural and periodic contexts.[15]

This broad divide within the study of magic between essentialism and linguisticism is similarly noted by Michael Bailey, who identifies on the one hand a "number of overarching theories and definitions" which tend to frame "magic" in distinction from either science or religion,[16] and on the other a trend which focuses "on historically and culturally specific understandings of magic" and operates under the aegis of the "careful examination of the words and concepts used to designate various magical actions."[17] Thus, in terms of this study, while an essentialist might concern themselves with answering questions such as "is θεαγωγία a magical or religious activity?"; a linguisticist might ask "does Iamblichus distinguish θεαγωγία as an activity apart from θεουργία?"

1.2.2 Essentialism in the Social Sciences

Essentialism in the study of magic both originated and has since maintained the greatest foothold in the social sciences. For one of its earliest proponents, Edward Tylor, magic exists among "the lowest known stages of civilization, and the lower races,

---

[10]Hammond, "Magic," 1349–56.
[11]Hanegraaff, *Esotericism and the Academy*, 164–77.
[12]Graf, *Magic in the Ancient World*, 2.
[13]Ogden, *Greek and Roman Necromancy*, xviii.
[14]Ibid.
[15]Ibid., xix.
[16]Bailey, "The Meanings of Magic," 3.
[17]Ibid., 5.

1.2. METHODOLOGY

who have not partaken largely in the education of the world" as a sort of proto-science.[18] This essentialised view of magic as a framework within which manifestations across all cultures could be charted and understood was paramount to the work of Sir James George Frazer. His opus, *The Golden Bough*, defined magic as the confluence of belief and behaviour operating in accord with the principle of universal sympathy. And, within this, Frazer subdivided two categories of "homeopathic" and "contagious" magic, operating under the respective laws of "similarity" and "contact" accordingly.[19]

Following in Frazer's wake, the torch of essentialism was carried onward by Émile Durkheim, whose work sought to distinguish magic from religion by defining the former as a socially atomised and intentionally heterodox transformation of the latter.[20] The task of universally defining "magic" was later taken up by Lynn Thorndyke, whose encyclopaedic *History of Magic and Experimental Science* begins by denoting as "magic" a nexus both of "ideas or doctrine" as well as "an operative art" that exists apart from the religious and scientific spheres.[21] This attitude in which "magic" can be construed as a universal category is further exemplified in the work of Bronislaw Malinowski, who upholds it as both "a mode of action as well as a system of belief" present among all peoples, which — similar to Thorndyke — is conceived of as distinct from both science and religion.[22] While this list of exemplars is far from exhaustive, it serves well to demonstrate the principle ways in which "magic" has been essentialised in modern scholarship.

1.2.3 Linguisticism and Philology

Opposition to essentialism has principally found advocates among classical philologists studying discourses on "magic" as it particularly pertains to the Graeco-Roman world. One of the earliest proponents of linguisticism as a counter approach to essential-

---

[18]Tylor, *Primitive Culture*, 1:112.
[19]Frazer, *The Golden Bough*, 12–14.
[20]Durkheim, *The Elementary Forms of the Religious Life* 42–44.
[21]Thorndike, *A History of Magic and Experimental Science*, 1:4.
[22]Malinowski, "Magic, Science, and Religion," 8.

ism was Alan Segal, who argued that "magic" is incapable of being used as an absolutely definable term "since all definitions of magic are relative to the culture and subculture under discussion."[23] In highlighting the relationship between magical practice and initiatory mystery religion in the *PGM*, Betz notes Segal's anti-essentialist objections and tentatively concurs, with particular criticism levelled at those theorists who would define "magic" in opposition to science and/or religion.[24] In relation to the particular problems posed by identifying the early Greek binding spells as falling under broader categories of "magic" or "religion," Christopher A. Faraone concludes that such essentialised headings are not "of any great help in analyzing and evaluating the peculiar cultural phenomena presented by the" curse tablets.[25] In his translation of a large number of curse tablets, John R. Gager notes his intentional avoidance of the term "magic," stating his "conviction that magic, as a definable and consistent category of human experience, simply does not exist," and which "tells us little or nothing about the substance of what is under description."[26] Linguisticist methodology is also applied by Matthew W. Dickie, who argues that essentialist projects of providing a definition "that will hold good for all cultures and that will at the same time explain what it is that all procedures thought of as magical have in common [...] are doomed to failure" on account of the facts that they both necessarily ignore the historical context that led to the emergence of Greek magic and that it is a prima facie error to assume "that all concepts have at their heart a core or essence."[27]

Linguisticist critiques of essentialism tend to resolve what they view as the inherent problems of the latter by means of an approach that is characterised less by universalism and generality, but rather by applying a careful focus on individual instantiations as they present themselves. Fritz Graf was an early proponent of this methodology. In his *Magic in the Ancient World*, Graf argues against the creation of "a rigid and artificial terminology"

---

[23] Segal, "Hellenistic Magic," 351.
[24] Betz, "Magic and Mystery in the Greek Magical Papyri," 244–47.
[25] Faraone, "The Agonistic Context of Early Greek Binding Spells," 20.
[26] Gager, "Introduction," 24–25.
[27] Dickie, *Magic and Magicians in the Greco-Roman World*, 18.

1.2. METHODOLOGY

— instead proposing that research into "magical" practices and beliefs be done by means of a "scrupulous analysis of the ancient terminology" of the Greeks themselves.[28] This methodological focus on the vocabulary of antique practitioners of "magic" is similarly followed by Jan N. Bremmer, who deems it "impossible to discuss the meaning of the terms *magos* and *mageia* for the whole of Antiquity" (much less throughout all time), owing to term's semantic mutability.[29] A similar approach is followed by Derek Collins, who explains that "the central dilemma for any student of Greek magic is that the Greek term *mageia* [...] only emerges in the latter half of the fifth century BCE while the evidence for practices and substances that we understood to be magical, as well as for individuals who were thought to be magicians, existed prior to the birth of the term."[30] For, as Collins details, the problem of attempting to impose an essentialised definition of "magic" across the Greek world is acutely evidenced by the fact that descriptions of actions that we would consider to be clearly magical (e.g. Circe turning Odysseus' men into swine in the *Odyssea*)[31] were not considered as instances of μαγεία during their composition prior to the entrance of "magical" terminology into the Greek vocabulary.[32]

In such an instance, is our understanding of Homer increased by retroactively applying a fifth century BC term to a text several centuries older? While it is true, as Collins notes, that an action of Odysseus' such as his summoning the soul of Tiresias[33] would have been clearly identified by fifth century BC audiences as an instance of ψυχαγωγία,[34] it does not necessarily follow suit that a seventh or eighth century audience would view his actions in the same light. Indeed, regarding these two episodes from the *Odyssea*, Dickie notes that even though we are culturally inclined to identify Circe as a "sorceress" or "witch," "it should be acknowledged that there is nothing in the Greek text to sug-

---

[28] Graf, *Magic in the Ancient World*, 18–19.
[29] Bremmer, "The Birth of the Term 'Magic,'" 1.
[30] Collins, *Magic in the Ancient Greek World*, 27.
[31] Homer, *The Odyssey*, X.203–43.
[32] Collins, *Magic in the Ancient Greek World*, 28
[33] Homer, *The Odyssey*, XI.90–149.
[34] Collins, *Magic in the Ancient Greek World*, p. 28.

gest that its author possessed the concept of magic and that he thought of Circe as a sorceress."[35] Similarly with Odysseus, although we are wont to see his actions as necromantic "magic," "there is no suggestion in the *Odyssey* that Odysseus is acting as a sorcerer."[36] To be sure, Homer identifies Circe here as having given Odysseus' men a φάρμακον (drug) — a word whose sense shifts fluidly between "magical" and medical senses in classical Greek.[37] However, it would not be until several centuries later, during the fifth century, that φαρμακεία, μαγεία, and γοητεία would be seen as largely synonymous.[38] This being the case, it would seem that a premature conflation of φαρμακεία with μαγεία under the classification of "magic" would serve to obfuscate rather than illuminate in the case of Homer.

In approaching the subject of discourses on "magic" within the late antique corpora, I believe that this can be better done by means of a careful and sensitive analysis of the terms used by the authors under discussion rather than by attempting to impose universal ideas of "magic" or "religion" upon the material.[39] As it particularly pertains to θεαγωγία within a late antique context, the use of philological methods seem to necessarily be the clearest choice, owing to the fact that its attestations occur within a range of works whose contents do not lend themselves readily to discrete classification as either "magical" or "religious" literature. Would essentialising θεαγωγία as being a either a "magical" or a "religious" practice in any way aid our understanding of the way in which it was viewed by the author of *PGM* IV.930–1113 or by Iamblichus? I do not believe so. On the contrary, such categorisations would assuredly hinder more than they would help.

As such, I have tended to avoid labelling specific practices as being "magical" (or "religious") whenever possible. For, in some

---

[35] Dickie, *Magic and Magicians*, 23.

[36] Dickie, *Magic and Magicians*, 22.

[37] *LSJ*, s.v. "φάρμακον," "φαρμακάω".

[38] Dickie, *Magic and Magicians*, 27–8; Collins, *Magic in the Ancient Greek World*, 28; Graf, *Magic in the Ancient World*, 28.

[39] This holds true for investigations into other corpora as well. I have previously utilized similar philologically based methodologies to analyze nineteenth and early twentieth century occult corpora. See: Plaisance, "Occult Spheres, Planes, and Dimensions," 385–404; Plaisance, "The Transvaluation of 'Soul' and 'Spirit,'" 250–72.

1.3. TERMS AND DEFINITIONS 9

instances, it is clear that θεαγωγία is used as a cognate to the "magical" practice of ψυχαγωγία, or the erotic ἀγωγή operations. Yet, in others, it is clearly described as more akin to "religious" θεουργία than anything else. And, given the fact that the very idea of "magic" as being "religion's opposite" may have "evolved out of tensions between pagan monotheism and daimonology," it seems that an understanding of such phenomena as θεαγωγία would benefit the greatest from interpretative models that do not presuppose the biases of its historical detractors.[40] This being the case, my analysis proceeds by means of documenting θεαγωγία and the related terminological apparatus as they are presented in each individual situation within the *PGM* and using this data to better comprehend its position within the proper historical context.

1.3 Terms and Definitions

1.3.1 Defining Θεαγωγία

To begin, a thorough linguistic breakdown of θεαγωγία will provide a useful starting point in the philological investigation that follows. The *Greek-English Lexicon* of Henry George Liddell and Robert Scott defines the verb θεαγωγέω as to "evoke gods," with θεαγωγία as the abstract noun designating the activity (the evocation of gods),[41] and θεαγωγός being the attested adjective indicating theagogic operations (e.g. θεαγωγὸς λόγος, a formula to evoke gods).[42] Following Charles Alexandre's lead,[43] Hans Lewy traces the word's origin as a combination of θεός (god) and "the magical term ἀγωγή."[44] Within a "magical" context, the *LSJ* defines ἀγωγή (pl. ἀγωγαί) as "evoking" and a "spell for bringing," noting its specific use as a "love-charm" thought to

---

[40] Fraser, "The Contested Boundaries of 'Magic' and 'Religion' in Late Pagan Monotheism," 131–51.
[41] *LSJ*, s.v. "θεαγωγέω."
[42] *LMPG*, s.v. "θεαγωγός." Muñoz defines θεαγωγός as "de una fórmula... que atrae a la divinidad."
[43] *Dictionnaire Grec-Français*, s.v. "θεαγωγός": "Θεαγωγός... qui évoque ou fait paraitre les dieux par ses enchantements. R.R. θεός, ἄγω."
[44] Lewy, *Chaldaean Oracles and Theurgy*, ff. 153.

draw the spell's target to the evocator.⁴⁵ In this way, the combination of θεός and ἀγωγή, come to indicate an operation in which a god is impelled towards the spell caster — an evocation of a god. This combination, where the -αγωγία stem is combined with a subject being compelled towards the evocator, can be seen as well in the terms ψυχαγωγία and φωταγωγία, which the *LSJ* translate as "conjuring up the dead"⁴⁶ and a "magical process of drawing down supernatural illumination"⁴⁷ respectively. In this way, we can view the dictionary definition of θεαγωγία as a being member of a family of operations who all share in common the intended goal of calling forth a subject, which is then drawn to the operator. While this synchronic definition is not necessarily what we will see extracted from the *PGM*, a baseline notion of the term's components and what it is generally thought to mean will benefit the exegesis.⁴⁸

The precise origin of the term θεαγωγία is difficult to determine. The two earliest attestations are divided into two groups: one, fragments attributed to Porphyry; two, spells from the so-called Great Magical Papyrus of Paris. The Porphyrian fragment first appears in Eusebius' (AD c. 260–c. 341) *Praeparatio evangelica*.⁴⁹ Although the diction differs slightly from the passage in *De mysteriis*,⁵⁰ Angelo Sodano identifies this fragment as being a direct quotation from Porphyry's *Epistula ad Anebonem* — the missive to which *De mysteriis* was a response.⁵¹ Additionally, the fragment is quoted verbatim in a later gloss on Chaeremon

---

⁴⁵*LSJ*, s.v. "ἀγωγή." The *LMPG* (s.v. "ἀναγωγή") concurs, defining ἀγωγή principally as "evocatión" (evocation) and secondarily as "encantamiento, fórmula para atraer a una persona, gener. con fines eróticos" (enchantment, formula to attract a person, generally for erotic purposes).

⁴⁶*LSJ*, s.v. "ψυχαγωγέω."

⁴⁷*LSJ*, s.v. "φωταγωγέω."

⁴⁸The distinction here between synchronic and diachronic approaches are derived from Ferdinand de Saussure's (1857–1913) work. For working definitions of the terms, see Normand, "System, Arbitrariness, Value," 93.: "By 'synchrony' Saussure was referring to a language (*une langue*) at a given time; by 'diachrony' he was referring to its various transformations throughout its history, reaching as far back as possible."

⁴⁹Eusebius, *Eusebius Werke VIII*, V.10.1–3.

⁵⁰Iamblichus, *On the Mysteries*, VI.1.241.

⁵¹Porphyry, *Porfirio*, 2.8a–b.

1.3. TERMS AND DEFINITIONS

of Alexandria's (1st century AD) *Fragmenta*[52] and Theodoret of Cyrus' (AD c. 393–c. 457) *Graecarum affectionum curatio*.[53] As *De mysteriis* was written at some point between AD 280 and 305,[54] it necessarily follows that Porphyry's epistle was composed shortly before that date.[55] While this dating of Porphyry's fragment is a relatively easy matter, the case is not so clear cut with the magical papyri. Estimated composition dates for the Paris papyrus, which comprises book IV of the *PGM*, vary widely. In his catalogue of Egyptian antiquities in France's Bibliothèque Nationale, François Lenormant estimated that the papyrus' writing could be dated to the second century AD.[56] However, the palaeographic analysis of the papyrus by Frederic Kenyon[57] and Albrecht Dieterich[58] estimate it to be a fourth century AD composition. The English language editor and translator of the *PGM*, Hans Dieter Betz, notes Lenormant's assessment, but ultimately concurs with the palaeographers.[59]

This broad date of *PGM* IV, however, does not entirely settle the matter of which attestation's tradition of usage is earliest. Although it seems somewhat more probable that Porphyry's fragment is slightly earlier, the nature of the Greek magical papyri as scribal compilations and rewritings of material from diverse hands makes it likely that the term θεαγωγία had some degree of currency among Graeco-Egyptian authors prior to the transcription of *PGM* IV. Additionally, since Porphyry's use is assuredly the first instance among any of the Neoplatonists, it is not unreasonable to conjecture that he may have encountered the term from a near Eastern author similar to those who composed the spells of the *PGM*, and then introduced it into Neoplatonic discourse. This argument in favor of an Egyptian origin is bolstered by the networks of similarities that exist between θεαγωγία and

---

[52] Chaeremon, *Fragmenta*, fr. 3.

[53] Theodoret, *Graecarum affectionum curatio*, III.66–67.

[54] Clarke, Dillon, and Hershbell, "Introduction," xxvii.

[55] For more on Porphyry's letter, see: Addey, *Divination and Theurgy in Neoplatonism*, 127–170; Smith, *Porphyry's Place in the Neoplatonic Tradition*, 83–99.

[56] Lenormant, *Catalogue d'une collections d'antiquités Égyptiennes*, 87.

[57] Kenyon, *The Palaeography of Greek Papyri*, 25.

[58] Dieterich, *Eine Mithrasliturgie*, 43–46.

[59] Betz, "Introduction," 8–9.

the Demotic *pḥ-nṯr*,⁶⁰ a category of spells within the *Papyri Demoticae magicae*⁶¹ whose goals are to summon a god into the operator's presence. What this seemingly ultimate origin in late antique Graeco-Egyptian practices means will be fully explored later. At the present, it suffices to note that the fact that θεαγωγία is closely connected with — both analogically and homologically — an older Egyptian term, which allows us to view the tradition of usage in the *PGM* as the source from which later instances can be ultimately derived.

1.3.2 Μαγεία and Γοητεία

Apart from the ἀγωγή family, there are three important words for "magic" that must be briefly discussed. The first is the term from which our English word "magic" is derived: μαγεία, the activity of the μάγος (pl. μάγοι).⁶² Attestations of μάγος long precede those of μαγεία, and the former's origin is firmly rooted in ancient Persia,⁶³ deriving from "the Old Persian name for the priest *magu-* (nom. *Maguš*) and is etymologically related to the Avestan *moyu-*, which seems to have meant '(member of a) tribe.'"⁶⁴ The term enters the Greek vocabulary with Heraclitus' (c. 535–c. 475 BC) obscure reference to: "νυκτιπόλος, μάγοις, βάκχοις, λήναις, μύσταις" (night-wanderers, Magi, Bacchantes, Maenads,

---

⁶⁰Dielman, "Scribal Practices in the Production of Magic Handbooks in Egypt," 108; Betz, "Introduction," 56.

⁶¹This appellation, *PDM*, strictly refers to the compilation in the *GMPT*, which is itself composed of four papyri: *PDM* XII, *PDM* XIV, *PDM* LXI, and the *PDM Supplement*. The Demotic editions of the first three papyri are found in: *The Demotic Magical Papyrus of London and Leiden*. The Demotic edition of the fourth papyrus is found in: Johnson, "Louvre E 3229," 55–102. For a general treatment of the Demotic papyri, see: Dielman, *Priests, Tongues, and Rites*.

⁶²For useful discussions of the etymology and origin of this term, see: Graf, *Magic in the Ancient World*, 20–21; Dickie, *Magic and Magicians*, 14; Bremmer, "The Birth of the Term 'Magic,'" 1–11; Collins, *Magic in the Ancient Greek World*, 54.

⁶³Graf, *Magic in the Ancient World*, 20–1; Dickie, *Magic and Magicians in the Greco-Roman World*, 14; Bremmer, "The Birth of the Term 'Magic,'" 1–2.

⁶⁴Collins, *Magic in the Ancient Greek World*, 54.

1.3. TERMS AND DEFINITIONS

[and] initiates).⁶⁵ What μάγος, in its early sense, appears to indicate is an itinerant priest who is associated with the performance of impious and unsanctioned initiation rituals.⁶⁶ There is likely a connection to the genuine Persian Magi here, but it is unclear whether Heraclitus is here referring to *bona fide* Persian fire-priests, charlatans passing themselves off as such, or is simply referring to wandering heterodox priests in general.⁶⁷ By the time we reach the fifth century BC, μάγος was commonly used to designate a class of men associated with a whole host of activities including: the casting of curse spells, the performance of unsanctioned mystery rites, the practice of exorcism, in addition to begging and juggling.⁶⁸

Towards the latter half of the fifth century, both the idea of what constituted a "magician" as well as societal views of "magic" were complicated by the identification of the μάγος with another figure: the γόης. Both the activity γοητεία and the performer of such, the γόης (pl. γόητες), translate equally as terms for "sorcery" (and "sorcerer") and "juggling" (and "juggler"),⁶⁹ and are etymologically connected to the term γόος, which was a "spontaneous and emotionally powerful" type of funerary lament.⁷⁰ It is in Gorgias (c. 485–c. 380 BC) that we first encounter μαγεία and γοητεία as paired terms describing the same "magic."⁷¹ Gorgias describes the pair as "δισσαὶ τέχναι" (two-fold arts), which are both "ψυχῆς ἁμαρτήματα" (faults, or sins, of the soul) and "δόξης

---

⁶⁵Heraclitus, *Fragmenta*, fr. 14. For a further exploration of this fragment, see: Lycourinos, "Those Who Wander in the Night," 55–74.

⁶⁶Dickie, *Magic and Magicians*, 28–29; Graf, *Magic in the Ancient World*, 21–22; Collins, *Magic in the Ancient Greek World*, 55.

⁶⁷Dickie, *Magic and Magicians*, 29. For more on the complex topic of Platonic orientalism, see: Hanegraaff, *Esotericism and the Academy*, 12ff.; Burns, "The Chaldean Oracles of Zoroaster, Hekate's Couch, and Platonic Orientalism in Psellos and Plethon," 158–79.

⁶⁸Graf, *Magic in the Ancient World*, 21–24; Dickie, *Magic and Magicians*, 33–36; Collins, *Magic in the Ancient Greek World*, 61.

⁶⁹*LSJ*, s.v. "γόης," "γοητεία."

⁷⁰Johnston, *Restless Dead*, 100–01; Graf, *Magic in the Ancient World*, 28; Dickie, *Magic and Magicians*, 13–14; Collins, *Magic in the Ancient Greek World*, 58–59.

⁷¹Graf, *Magic in the Ancient World*, 26; Collins, *Magic in the Ancient Greek World*, 58.

ἀπατήματα" (deceptions of opinions).[72] Gorgias describes their art as effected by "ἐπῳδαὶ" (incantations),[73] which is quite similar to the way Plato (c. 427–c. 347 BC) depicts the art.[74] He details the ways in which people believe themselves to be the victims of "μαγγανείας" (trickery, *LSJ* notes it is used "esp. of magical arts"),[75] "ἐπῳδαῖς" (incantations), and "καταδέσεσι" (magical binding), or of coming under the influence of "δυναμένων γοητεύειν" (the power to bewitch or enchant). There is also a great deal of evidence to connect γοητεία to ψυχαγωγία, as Sarah Iles Johnston and Ogden have demonstrated.[76]

These wandering mendicant figures became the focus of a great deal of discussion by philosophers in the fourth century BC. The Hippocratic treatise, *De morbo sacro*, levels what Collins describes as "arguably the most influential attack on magic ever made in antiquity."[77] The text describes the μάγοι as being ἀγύρται (beggars), ἀλαζονίας (quacks), and men who falsely claim to be both "σφόδρα θεοσεβέες" (exceedingly pious, or god-fearing) and "πλέον τι εἰδέναι" (filled with knowledge).[78] This false-knowledge and false-piety is, according to the author, exemplified by the ways in which the μάγοι interact with the gods. This charge of impiety against them is formulated in two parts. First, it proceeds by identifying natural phenomena and bodies such as the sun, moon, etc. as divine beings. Second, it charges that the manipulation of these phenomena by means of μαγεύω (the use of magical arts) necessarily bespoke of μάγοι who *either* disbelieved in the existence of the gods and were thus charlatans, *or* were so impious as to believe themselves capable of commanding the gods themselves.[79] A similar argument against these groups is made by Plato, who posits that the ἀγύρται and μάντεις (seers) are able to use "ἐπαγωγαῖς τισιν καὶ καταδέσμοις" (enchantments

---

[72] Gorgias, *Fragmenta*, fr. 10.
[73] Ibid.
[74] Plato, *Leges*, 933a–b.
[75] *LSJ*, s.v. "μαγγανάριος."
[76] Johnston, *Restless Dead*, 102–23; Ogden, *Greek and Roman Necromancy*, 95–115.
[77] Collins, *Magic in the Ancient Greek World*, 33.
[78] *The Sacred Disease*, I.2.1–10.
[79] *The Sacred Disease*, I.4.1–21. See also Collins, *Magic in the Ancient Greek World*, 31–36.

1.3. TERMS AND DEFINITIONS

and binding spells) to constrain the wills of the gods into serving them.[80] These begging seers are identified with the μάγοι and γόητες of Plato's *Leges*,[81] bringing his critiques of μαγεία and γοητεία more or less in line with that of the author of *De morbo sacro*.

1.3.3 Θεουργία

1.3.3.1 Origins of Θεουργία

This fourth century charge, that μαγεία and γοητεία were ultimately impious modes of interacting with the gods, was taken quite seriously by subsequent generations of Platonic philosophers, who resolved the problem several hundred years later with the introduction of what they deemed a thoroughly pious form of "magic" into their praxis: θεουργία.[82] The history of the introduction of the term θεουργία into Greek philosophical discourse is inextricably bound to the *Oracula Chaldaica*, "a collection of abstruse, hexameter verses purported to have been 'handed down by the gods' (θεοπαράδοτα) to a certain Julian the Chaldean and/or his son, Julian the Theurgist" at some point during the second century AD.[83] The *Oracula Chaldaica*, along with certain texts attributed to Orpheus, soon became viewed as sacred books within many Neoplatonic circles.[84] According to Marinus of Neapolis' (fifth century AD) *Vita Procli sive de felicitate*, the importance of the *Oracula Chaldaica* was such that it was through their study that Proclus was led to the "ἀκροτάτας τῶν ἀρετῶν" (the highest virtue) which had been dubbed "θεουργικὰς" (theur-

---

[80] Plato, *Respvblica*, 364b–c.
[81] Ogden, *Greek and Roman Necromancy*, 106.
[82] For general treatments of θεουργία, see: Athanassiadi, "The Chaldean Oracles," 115–30; Shaw, *Theurgy and the Soul*; Shaw, "Theurgy," 1–28; Shaw, "After Aporia," 57–82; Marx-Wolf, "High Priests of the Highest God," 481–513; Dodds, "Theurgy and Its Relationship to Neoplatonism," 55–57; Lewy, *Chaldaean Oracles and Theurgy*, 461–65; Johnston, *Hekate Soteira*; Tanaseanu-Döbler, *Theurgy in Late Antiquity*; Dillon, "Iamblichus' Defense of Theurgy," 30–41.
[83] Majercik, "Introduction," 1. For more on Julian the Theurgist, see Tanaseanu-Döbler, *Theurgy in Late Antiquity*, 137; Athanassiadi, *Mutations of Hellenism in Late Antiquity*, 193–208.
[84] Johnston, *Hekate Soteira*, p. 4.

gic),[85] and from the "μυχρῶν μυστηρίων" (lesser mysteries) to the greater Platonic mysteries.[86]

As Ruth Majercik notes, "although the precise term θεουργία does not appear in the extant fragments, the related noun θεουργοί [theurgists] does."[87] In what is the earliest attestation of theurgic terminology, the *Oracula* describe the θεουργοί (sing. θεουργός) as being unbound by "εἱμαρτὴν" (destiny, or fate).[88] Outside of the *Oracula Chaldaica* themselves, the practice of θεουργία gained the most currency within Neoplatonism. Although it is likely that the first bona fide Neoplatonist, Plotinus (AD c. 204–270), was aware of θεουργία as a religious technology being utilised by Middle Platonic predecessors, it appears to be the case that he disapproved of its practice, preferring instead the advocacy of strictly contemplative methods of shortening the gap between man and the gods.[89] It was, rather, through the works of Iamblichus that θεουργία became fully integrated into Neoplatonism.[90] Its importance being so great to the subject of this monograph's analysis, Iambichus, it behooves us to delve deeper into what θεουργία was thought of as being, and how it was thought to relate to such other forms of "magic" as μαγεία and γοητεία.

1.3.3.2 Σύστασις

Within the *Oracula Chaldaica*, we see θεουργία exemplified by three component practices: σύστασις (conjunction, or communication), τελεστική (statue animation), and ἀναγωγή (ascension).[91] Σύστασις, the first theurgic practice, is defined by Johnston as "any contact between theurgist and god, including mediu-

---

[85] Marinus, *Vita di Proclo*, 26.624–6.
[86] Marinus, *Vita di Proclo*, 13.320–3.
[87] Majercik, "Introduction," 21.
[88] *The Chaldean Oracles*, fr. 153.
[89] Johnston, *Hekate Soteira*, 79.
[90] Cf. Shaw, *Theurgy and the Soul*. For a complete list of synonyms for θεουργία used by Iamblichus, see: Tanaseanu-Döbler, *Theurgy in Late Antiquity*, 97–8.
[91] Johnston, *Hekate Soteira*, 87–89; Majercik, "Introduction," 21–46.

mistic possession or epiphany."⁹² Although the term only occurs once in the *Oracula Chaldaica* (and in a questionable fragment at that),⁹³ it is commonly found in the theurgic vocabularies both of Neoplatonists such as Proclus,⁹⁴ as well as the *PGM*.⁹⁵ For the purposes of this study, σύστασις is of particular import owing to its synonymity with θεαγωγία and *ph-ntr* within the Greek and Demotic magical papyri.⁹⁶ The picture that emerges from the context of these texts is that σύστασις was conceived of as a practice by which the θεουργός could either invoke a god, conjoining with it himself, or evocate a god, effecting its manifestation external to himself.

An interesting example of σύστασις in antiquity is found in Eunapius' (fourth to fifth century AD) *Vitae sophistarum*, where he describes Iamblichus' evocation of two daemons before a group of his students.⁹⁷ The party had gone to Gadara, a locale in Syria renowned for its hot baths. While there, Iamblichus' students began pestering him to work some wonder or another. Eunapius reports that, in a rare display, Iamblichus assented. At two different springs, he evocated two daemons — Eros and Anteros — (who were presumably thought to be guardians of their respective springs rather than the gods of love from Aphrodite's retinue), both of whom appeared as golden-haired youths and were clearly visible to his stupified pupils, all of whom were soundly stunned into silence by the display.

1.3.3.3 Τελεστική

Τελεστική, the second theurgic practice, is defined by Todd C. Krulak as a "ritual aspect of theurgy in which a god is invited into

---

⁹²Johnston, *Hekate Soteira*, 88. For more on σύστασις as possession, see: Addey, "Divine Possession and Divination in the Graeco-Roman World," 171–185.

⁹³Majercik, "Introduction," 25; *The Chaldean Oracles*, fr. 208: "For (Proclus) made use of the 'conjunctions' [συστάσεσι], prayers, and the divine, ineffable, magic wheels of the Chaldeans" (trans. Majercik).

⁹⁴Proclus, *In Platonis rem publicam commentarii*, II.11.18.

⁹⁵*PGM*, III.197, III.494, IV.779, IV.930, VI.1, VI.39.

⁹⁶Dielman, "Scribal Practices in the Production of Magic Handbooks in Egypt," 108; Ritner, "Egyptian Magical Practice Under the Roman Empire," 3346.

⁹⁷Eunapius, *Lives of the Philosophers and Sophists*, 368–73.

a ritual image thereby 'ensouling' (ἐμψυχός) or 'animating' it."[98] While the precise term τελεστική is not present in the attested fragments, it is found in several of the framing texts within which the fragments have been identified.[99] Additionally, the *Oracula Chaldaica* contains a fragmentary discourse given by Hecate to the θεουργός, describing how he might craft a statue which is fit for her to descend into and animate.[100] Descriptions of τελεστική are plentiful in antiquity, and are further found in Middle Platonic texts such as the *PGM*,[101] *Corpus Hermeticum*,[102] and *Asclepius*,[103] as well as in the works of later Neoplatonists such as Iamblichus,[104] Julian the Apostate (AD c. 331–363),[105] Syrianus (fifth century AD),[106] Proclus,[107] and Hermias (AD c. 410–c. 450).[108]

Perhaps the most picturesque example of τελεστική in Greek literature is relayed also by Eunapius, where he described the animation of a statue of Hecate.[109] Therein, he tells the story of Eusebius (not the Bishop) who was brought to a ceremony by Maximus of Ephesus (AD c. 310–372). Maximus invited Eusebius and the rest of the company into the temple, and after they were seated, burned incense and recited a hymn to the goddess. Eunapius reports Maximius' invocation being so successful that the Hecate's statue seemed to smile and laugh aloud. This disturbed the onlookers, at which Maximus implored them to not be frightened, lest the goddess ignite the statue's torches. And, with perfect dramatic timing, no sooner were Maximus' words spoken than the statue's torches erupted in gouts of flame.

---

[98]Krulak, "The Animated Statue and the Ascension of the Soul," xiii. For general information, see also: Lewy, *Chaldaean Oracles and Theurgy*, 495–96; Johnston, "Animating Statues," 445–77; Haluszka, "Sacred Signified," 479–94; Voss, "The Secret Life of Statues," 201–28.

[99] *The Chaldean Oracles*, ffr. 110, 136, 196.

[100] *The Chaldean Oracles*, fr. 224.

[101] *PGM*, V.370–421.

[102] *Corpus Hermeticum*, XVII.8–13.

[103] *Asclepius*, 24.

[104]Iamblichus, *On the Mysteries*, V.23.233–34.

[105]Julian, *Fragments of a Letter to a Priest*, 293a–294c.

[106]Proclus, *In Platonis Timaeum Commentarii.*, ffr. 2, 20.

[107]Proclus, *De sacrificio et magia*, 148–51.

[108]Hermias, *Hermiae Alexandri in Platonis Phaedrum scholia*, 87.5–13.

[109]Eunapius, *Lives*, 434–5.

1.3. TERMS AND DEFINITIONS

1.3.3.4 Ἀναγωγή

Ἀναγωγή, the third and final theurgic practice, is described by Johnston as "the primary goal of the theurgist" and "the temporary raising of his soul to the 'intellectual fire' of the noetic realm while the body was still alive."[110] And again, although the specific verbiage does not survive in any of the attested oracular fragments, ἀναγωγή is "clearly a Chaldean teaching."[111] The general scheme of anagogic practice that can be gleaned from the *Oracula Chaldaica* revolves around the notion that the "ψυχῆς λεπτὸν ὄχημα" (subtle vehicle of the soul)[112] could be made by the θεουργός to ascend from materiality towards the realm of the noetic gods by a purificatory process whereby the soul was enflamed with a "ἀχράντου πυρὸς" (pure fire)[113] that effected the act of "ἐμπέλασις" (approaching) the gods.[114] Like τελεστική, ἀναγωγή is found both in Middle Platonic texts such as the *Corpus Hermeticum*[115] and the *PGM*,[116] as well as in the works of Neoplatonists like Iamblichus.[117]

While many of the later Neoplatonists touted the efficacy of anagogic ascent, it is in the section of the *PGM* known as the "Mithras Liturgy," that we find the most vivid first-hand account of the process.[118] Therein, the author describes ascending upwards into the sky, to behold the visible gods (i.e. the planets) — all of whom appear by passing through a hollow tube which proceeds from the Sun. What follows then is a series of interac-

---

[110] Johnston, *Hekate Soteira*, 89.

[111] Majercik, "Introduction," 30.

[112] *The Chaldean Oracles*, fr. 120. For general information on the doctrine of the ὄχημα and its connection to ἀναγωγή, see: Kissling, "The Οχημα-Πνευμα of the Neo-Platonists and the *De Insomniis* of Synesius of Cyrene," 318–30; Finamore, *Iamblichus and the Theory of the Vehicle of the Soul*; Schibli, "Hierocles of Alexandria and the Vehicle of the Soul," 109–17.

[113] *The Chaldean Oracles*, fr. 122.

[114] *The Chaldean Oracles*, fr. 121.

[115] *Corpus Hermeticum*, I.24–26.

[116] *PGM*, IV.537–57.

[117] Iamblichus, *De mysteriis*, X.6.

[118] *PGM*, IV.475–829. For a full exegesis of this curious text and the possibility of its having a relationship with historical Mithraism, the most complete account is: Betz, *The "Mithras Liturgy"*. For an ethnographic account of the ritual, see: Lycourinos, *Ritual Embodiment in Modern Western Magic*, 103–16.

tions between the ascended author, the text's central god Helios Mithras Aion, and various classes of planetary beings.

1.3.4 "Magical" Disjunctions

Despite E.R. Dodds' assertion that "the creator of theurgy was a magician,"[119] it was a common rhetorical tactic for θεουργοί — particularly Neoplatonists — to distinguish their praxis from that of the μάγοι and γόητες. While "theurgy shared certain methodologies with γοητεία [...] its primary goal — the ascent of the soul and its unification with the divine — definitely differed from the γόητες," whose aims were generally more prosaic and materially oriented.[120] While we see no instances of these two "magical" terms in the *Oracula Chaldaica*, the two earliest Neoplatonic θεουργοί very clearly describe a disjunction between θεουργία and γοητεία. In Porphyry's case, Augustine (AD 354–430) reports him as defining *theurgia* as the "purgationem animae" (purification of the soul),[121] and notes that he thought of it as existing in contradistinction to the "detestabiliore" (detestable) acts of *magia* and *goetia*.[122] Additionally, in his *Epistula ad Anebonem*, Porphyry contrasts the impious "ἀγύρτας καὶ ἀλαζόντας" (beggars and quacks) — whom we have previously seen identified with μάγοι and γόητες — against the "θεῶν θεραπευτάς" (worshippers of the gods) and practitioners of "ἀληθινῆς θεολογίας" (true theology) and "θεουργίας" (theurgy).[123] Moving on to Iamblichus, as Gregory Shaw notes, he "argued that theurgy had nothing to do with sorcery," as the former proceeds by means of subordinating human will to that of the divine — whereas the latter inverted this relationship, attempting to subordinate the divine to the human.[124] In *De mysteriis*, Iamblichus specifically warns us against comparing the "ἐνέργειαν ἱερατικαῖς

---

[119] Dodds, "Theurgy," 57.
[120] Johnston, *Hekate Soteira*, 87.
[121] Augustine, *De civitate Dei*, X.9.18.
[122] Augustine, *De citivate Dei*, X.9.10–11. However, in what is likely an eisegetical interpolation, Augustine notes (*De civitate Dei*, X.9.18–19) that Porphyry's defense of *theurgia* is characterized by "cunctanter [...] et pudibunda" (reluctance and shame).
[123] Porphyry, *Epistula ad Anebonem*, 18d.1–3.
[124] Shaw, "Theurgy," 1.

1.3. TERMS AND DEFINITIONS

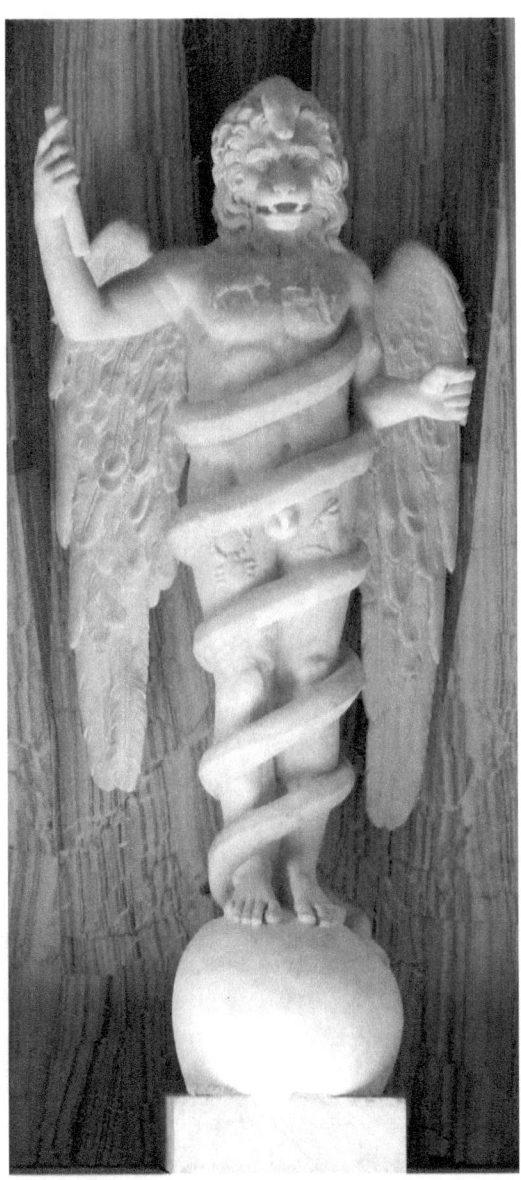

Figure 1.1: A statue of a leontocephaline Mithraic deity, similar to Helios Mithras Aion as described in *PGM* IV.475–829, from the Vatican Museum's collection. Photo by Vassil, 2017.

τῶν θεῶν ὄψεσιν" (visions of the gods from hieratic operations) with the "φαντασίαις" (images) produced artificially by "γοητείας τεχνικῶς" (arts of magic).[125]

While it, thus, seems clear that the γόης and θεουργός were conceived of as intrinsically separate figures by antique authors, the distinction is not quite as clear cut when looking at the μάγος. For instance, the *PGM* utilize the term "ἱερᾶς μαγείας" (holy magic)[126] — which clearly calls to mind θεουργία and its divine orientation — within the context of a spell which Damon Zacharias Lycourinos describes as a mystery rite designed to transform the initiate.[127] However, the spell identifies itself as having the power to "πείθειν θεοὺς καὶ πάσας τὰς θεάς" (persuade all the gods and goddesses),[128] which, as Betz notes, places it squarely within the "old literary definition of magic as persuading gods."[129] Thus, we arrive at a nebulous situation in which the text in question displays characteristic attributes of "magical" and "theurgic" texts at once. The *Suda* as well, makes a rather interesting distinction between γοητεία and μαγεία that is pertinent to the present discussion. The text describes μαγεία and γοητεία as inherently "διαφέρουσιν" (different) things. It portrays μαγεία as the "ἐπίκλησις" (invocation) of "δαιμόνων ἀγαθοποιῶν" (benevolent daemons), and γοητεία as "ἀνάγειν" (raising) the dead also by means of "ἐπικλήδεως" (invocation).[130] In this case, then, we see a clearer instance of μαγεία coming to be used to designate a "good magic" that bears similarities to θεουργία, and γοητεία as an "evil magic" that is more in line with early antique conceptions of both μαγεία and γοητεία. What these instances begin to demonstrate is that there was, throughout antiquity, not a single, stable, immutable perceived relationship between γοητεία, μαγεία, and θεουργία. To be sure, there were broad trends, but the fact that the precise meanings of these terms underwent

---

[125] Iamblichus, *On the Mysteries*, III.25.160.

[126] *PGM*, I.127.

[127] Lycourinos, "The Spell of Pnouthis as a Mystery Rite in the Greek Magical Papyri," 19–32.

[128] *PGM*, I.53–54.

[129] Betz, "The Formation of Authoritative Tradition in the Greek Magical Papyri," 175.

[130] *Sudiae lexicon*, s.v. "γοητεία."

subtle shifts and changes as they passed from author to author should caution us against approaching their historical study by any means that treat those terms — of their English translations — as having absolute meanings.

Chapter 2

Spells of Binding and Constraint

2.1 Κατάδεσμοι and *Defixiones*

2.1.1 Curse Tablets in the Graeco-Roman World

The erotic ἀγωγαί spells, with which θεαγωγία itself appears most deeply connected, "developed historically out of the Greek tradition of binding spells"[1] — the primary function of which was to influence, against their will (and generally without their knowledge), the actions and/or welfare of external parties by means of supernatural intercession.[2] As an understanding of this tradition of binding spells, κατάδεσμοι, will allow us to contextualise the compulsory natures of both the ἀγωγαί spells and θεαγωγία operations, some background on the topic will prove useful in framing the central discussion. In keeping with the overriding linguisticist methodology, insight into what the κατάδεσμοι were, and what kinds of implicit metaphysical ideas are present can best be obtained by analysing the specific words used both to refer to the acts of binding and within the tablets themselves. As previously mentioned, the respective Greek and Latin terms for these curse

---

[1] Faraone, *Ancient Greek Love Magic*, 143. For the general connection between ἀγωγαί spells and κατάδεσμοι, see: Winkler, "The Constraints of Eros," 231.

[2] Jordan, "A Survey of Greek Defixiones Not Included in the Special Corpora," 151.

tablets were κατάδεσμος and *defixio* (pl. *defixiones*).³ Among the Greek tablets, the dominant verb used to connote the act of binding was καταδέω, to which the Latin *defigo* is both homonymous and synonymous.⁴ The literal meaning of καταδέω is "to bind on, or to" or "to bind fast," an action fundamentally concerned with coercive constraint.⁵ And, it is precisely this sense of forcefully binding something against its will that the words carry when used metaphorically within the context of the curse tablets. There were many other active verbs found within the κατάδεσμοι, but the general connotation of forceful coercion is a constant.⁶ There is more to be said about some of the linguistic specifics of the κατάδεσμοι insofar as they pertain to the implied relationship between the operator and the gods, but more will be made of that in the next chapter.

Κατάδεσμοι represent "arguably the most widely employed kinds of magic" in the antique world — a fact exemplified not only by the large number of extant curse tablets, but also copious second-hand accounts in period literature.⁷ The number of κατάδεσμοι is difficult to pin down with precision. Of the four principal published corpora, Richard Wünsch's *Defixionum tabellae Atticae* contains 220 Greek curse tablets; Augustus Audollent's *Defixionum tabellae* attempted to flesh out the corpus and presented 305 spells in both Greek and Latin; D.R. Jordan's survey of κατάδεσμοι not included either in Wünsch or Audollent adds another 650;⁸ finally, Jordan's subsequent survey introduces 122 more instances to the corpus.⁹ This gives us a rough estimate of just under 1,300 curse tablets that have been presented

---

³Faraone, "The Agonistic Context of Early Greek Binding Spells," 3; Collins, *Magic in the Ancient Greek World*, 64.

⁴Audollent, "Prooemium," lv–lvi; Graf, *Magic in the Ancient World*, 125; Faraone, "The Agonistic Context of Early Greek Binding Spells," 21; Dickie, *Magic and Magicians*, 17.

⁵*LSJ*, s.v. "καδαδέω."

⁶The most comprehensive list of curse verbs can be found in: Audollent, "Prooemium," lvii–lix. A useful abbreviated list is also in: Graf, *Magic in the Ancient World*, 125.

⁷Collins, *Magic in the Ancient Greek World*, 64.

⁸Jordan, "A Survey of Greek *Defixiones* Not Included in the Special Corpora."

⁹Jordan, "New Greek Curse Tablets (1985–2000)," 5–46

2.1. ΚΑΤΑΔΕΣΜΟΙ AND DEFIXIONES

in major publications thus far,[10] which is a tremendously large number of instances of a single genre of inscriptions.

2.1.2 Curse Tablet Materials

The popularity of the κατάδεσμοι is further evidenced by references in a broad range of antique literature.[11] Perhaps the earliest evidence for the ubiquity of binding spells in the antique world is Aeschylus' (c. 525–c. 456 BC) *Eumenides*, where he describes a "δέσμιον" (binding spell)[12] whose function is that of "δέσμιος φρενῶν" (binding the mind, or heart).[13] However, it is in Plato that we see the greatest detail. In *Respublica*, the "καταδέσμοις" (binding spells) mentioned earlier can be tied to his discussion in *Leges*, where he ponders what ought to be the legal ramifications of "καταδέσεσι" (binding spells) which operate by means of such things as waxen images deposited as doorways, crossroads, or in graveyards.[14] This combination of evidence both among the binding tablets themselves, and references which treat them as commonplace in literature of the same period work together to paint a picture of a practice which was widespread throughout the Graeco-Roman world at the time.

The κατάδεσμοι appear to have become popular throughout the Mediterranean during the fifth century BC, as the oldest caches of tablets date to that period.[15] The oldest examples — which have been found in Sicily, Olbia, and Attica — can be reliably dated to this period, and "by the second century AD they begin turning up in every corner of the Greco-Roman world."[16]

---

[10] Ogden estimates that the total number of surviving κατάδεσμοι "found throughout the Graeco-Roman world, from Egypt to Britain" approaches 1,600: Ogden, *Magic, Witchcraft, and Ghosts in the Greek and Roman Worlds*, 210. Gager confirms this estimate, noting that "the total number of surviving examples exceeds fifteen hundred": Gager, "Introduction," 3.

[11] Graf, *Magic in the Ancient World*, 119–20.

[12] Aeschylus, *Eumenides*, 306.

[13] Ibid., 332.

[14] Plato, *Leges*, 933a–b.

[15] Jordan, "A Survey of Greek *Defixiones* Not Included in the Special Corpora," 151.

[16] Faraone, "The Agonistic Context of Early Greek Binding Spells," 3. Dickie (*Magic and Magicians*, 17) clarifies this, noting that "the earliest surviving lead tablets have been found in Selinus on the south-west coast

One of the reasons that such a large number of καταδεσμοι have managed to survive is due to the material into which they were inscribed: small sheets of beaten-out lead, which were then rolled up, pierced with a nail, and then often buried in either a cemetery or in a sanctuary to a chthonic deity.[17] These lead tablets were, according to Gager, relatively easy to inscribe, given the soft nature of the thin sheets.[18] And, as he notes, in *PGM* VII, a scribe detailing how to make a καταδεσμος notes that the lead ought to be inscribed by means of a bronze stylus.[19] This ease of inscription was, apparently, not the only reason for its widespread use. On the one hand, it was, at the time, very cheap and easy to obtain.[20] The above noted καταδεσμος from the *PGM* even goes so far as to steal the required amount of lead from a public water pipe.[21]

On the other hand, it seems that there were technical reasons why the tablets' creators might prefer lead over other easily inscribable materials. Graf and Faraone both note that the perceptions of lead as being without value, having no luster, and being characterised by coldness may have been seen by the creators of the καταδεσμοι as analogical properties which made lead particularly suitable for cursing their opponents (an operative theory about which more will be said later).[22] Lead was not, however, the only material from which curse tablets were crafted. Faraone notes Ovid's (43 BC–c. 17 AD) description of a wax *defixio*,[23] but explains that the harsh Aegean climate naturally precluded

---

of Sicily. They are to be dated to the early fifth century and come from a cemetery or from the sanctuary of Demeter Malophoros."

[17] Gager, "Introduction," 3; Graf, *Magic in the Ancient World*, 118; Dickie, *Magic and Magicians*, 17; Faraone, "The Agonistic Context of Early Greek Binding Spells," 3; Collins, *Magic in the Ancient Greek World*, 64; Ogden, *Magic, Witchcraft, and Ghosts in the Greek and Roman Worlds*, 210; Jordan, "A Survey of Greek *Defixiones* Not Included in the Special Corpora," 151.

[18] Gager, "Introduction," 4.

[19] *PGM*, VII.396–404.

[20] Faraone, "The Agonistic Context of Early Greek Binding Spells," 7.

[21] *PGM*, VII.396–404.

[22] Graf, *Magic in the Ancient World*, 132–33; Faraone, "The Agonistic Context of Early Greek Binding Spells," 7.

[23] Ovid, *The Amores*, III.7.27–30: "Num mea Thessalico languent devota veneno corpora? num misero carmen et herba nocent, sagave poenicea defixit nomina cera et medium tenuis in iecur egit acus?"

2.1. ΚΑΤΑΔΕΣΜΟΙ AND DEFIXIONES

the survival of any such wax tablets. However, given Ovid's account and the fact that such wax curse tablets have survived in Egypt's "more stable climate," it is likely that wax was, alongside lead, a common material from which κατάδεσμοι were made.[24] Additionally, according to Faraone and Gager,[25] *DTA* 55a — a fifth century BC κατάδεσμος found in Attica — specifically curses the victim both "ἐν μολύβδωι καὶ ἐν κηρῷ" (in lead and in beeswax),[26] lending further credence to the notion that wax was at least a somewhat commonly used base material.

The final point to be made in speaking of the materials from which κατάδεσμοι were crafted is that of the figurines and miniature statues which are often connected to the tablets. These figurines — commonly made from such materials as lead, wax, wool, clay, bronze, and marble — most often took the shape of a man or woman whose limbs were either bound, twisted, or otherwise intentionally disfigured.[27] The previously noted passage from Plato's *Leges* describes wax figurines as being an essential part of the cursing apparatus,[28] as do many of the formularies within the PGM which describe the process of producing κατάδεσμοι.[29] And indeed, this literary description has been confirmed by "a significant number of such figurines" which have been excavated.[30] Often, such binding figurines would have affixed to them something signifying the οὐσία (essence) of the intended victim — hair, fingernails, a piece of fabric from their clothing, etc. — and "in rare finds from Egyptian graves," such figurines have been discovered alongside the κατάδεσμοι with which they are connected.[31] And, as John J. Winkler notes,[32] not only does the *PGM* contain instructions for utilising οὐσία in the constructions of binding figurines,[33] but several of the papyri "were actually found wrapped

---

[24] Faraone, "The Agonistic Context of Early Greek Binding Spells," 7.
[25] Ibid.; Gager, "Introduction," 31.
[26] *DTA*, 55a.16–17.
[27] Collins, *Magic in the Ancient World*, 64; Gager, "Introduction," 15.
[28] Plato, *Leges*, 933a–b.
[29] For characteristic instances, see: *PGM* IV.296–466, IV.1716–1870, XII.14–95.
[30] Gager, "Introduction," 15.
[31] Graf, *Magic in the Ancient World*, 139.
[32] John J. Winkler, "The Constraints of Eros," 224.
[33] *PGM*, VII.462–66.

in hair."[34]

2.1.3 Creators of the Curse Tablets

Before delving into the underlying theory and specific practices associated with the κατάδεσμοι, it will prove useful to consider who their creators were. As the tablets themselves do not generally identify their creators as belonging to one or another of the classes of "magicians" we have thus far touched upon, an understanding of how they were viewed may be gleaned from comparisons with cognate texts and literary descriptions. Gager describes the professional class responsible for the curse tablets' inscription as "*magoi* or scribes," comparing the "highly formulaic texts" to the collections of similar formularies in the *PGM*.[35] Keeping in mind the commonly perceived identity between the μάγοι and γόητες during the fifth and fourth centuries BC — the period associated with the earliest caches of κατάδεσμοι — we may view Dickie's assertion that the creation of curse tablets "fell within the province of the *goes*" as being in line with Gager's statement.[36] In support of his position, Dickie references a fragment from Pherecydes of Athens (fifth century BC),[37] identifying the γόητες mentioned as creators of the κατάδεσμοι.[38] As Pherecydes' text does not specifically use any of the technical terminology associated with κατάδεσμοι, Dickie's link remains tenuous.

However, there are at least two literary instances which definitively identify the creator of the curse tablets as a γόης. First, is the Roman historian, Cassius Dio (AD c. 150–c. 235), who compared the way in which Cleopatra (69–30 BC) metaphorically enslaved ("ἐδεδούλωτο") Marcus Antonius (83–30 BC) to "μαγγανείας" (enchantment, with specific connotations of "magical" trickery)[39] — noting that she both "ἐγοήτευσε" (enchanted) and "κατέδησεν" (bound) him.[40] While this passage can certainly not

---

[34] He gives the following as examples: *PGM*, XVI, XIXa, LXXXIV.

[35] Gager, "Introduction," 5.

[36] Dickie, *Magic and Magicians*, 48.

[37] Pherecydes of Athens, "Pherekydes of Athens (Fragments 1–89)."

[38] Dickie, *Magic and Magicians*, 32, 48.

[39] Cassius Dio, *Cassii Dionis Cocceiani historiarum Romanarum quae supersunt*, L.5.1.

[40] Ibid., L.5.3–4.

2.2. THEORY AND PRACTICE

be taken as evidence that Cleopatra was literally thought to be connected with κατάδεσμοι or γοητεία, what it does indicate is a popular perception that the two categories were — if not identical — essentially linked. The second passage which makes a similar connection is from Plotinus (c. AD 204/5–270). As he answers the question of how "γοητείας" (magic spells) work,[41] Plotinus describes their activities as "ἐπαγωγαῖς" (evocation spells) and "καταδέσμοις" (binding spells).[42] Furthermore, as Plotinus equates γοητεία with μαγεία,[43] we may infer that his drawn link between the γόης and the κατάδεσμοι holds true for the μάγος as well. While the matter of ἀγωγή and ἐπαγωγή spells will be dealt with below, what we immediately gain from Plotinus is a solid instance of the identification of the γόητες and μάγοι as the creators of the κατάδεσμοι.

2.2 Theory and Practice

2.2.1 Functional Classification

In our discussion of κατάδεσμοι thus far, several points have been raised that merit further discussion within a deeper understanding of how such curses were believed to function — particularly the compulsory verb forms and the matter of the accompanying figurines. While it is clear that κατάδεσμοι in general expressed "a formalized wish to bring other persons or animals under the client's power,"[44] the kinds of bindings and the ways in which these bindings were believed to occur can be classified in several ways. Drawing on Audollent's early classificatory efforts,[45] Graf groups the κατάδεσμοι into the following five functional cat-

---

[41] Plotinus, *Enneads*, IV.4.40.1.

[42] Ibid., IV.4.40.19.

[43] Ibid., IV.4.40.1–6. For more general information on Plotinus' attitudes towards γοητεία and μαγεία in the *Enneades*, see: Merlan, "Plotinus and Magic," 341–48; Armstrong, "Was Plotinus a Magician?" 73–79; Clark, "Plotinus," 215–31.

[44] Gager, "Introduction," 21; Helleman, "Plotinus and Magic," 114–46.

[45] Audollent, "Prooemium," xc: "Quae si consideraveris tabellas in hunc fere modum distribuas. Tabellae iudiciariae et in inimicos conscriptae... in fures calumniatores et maledicos conversae... amatorie... in agitatores et venatores immissae."

egories: (1) judicial spells, (2) amatory spells, (3) agonistic spells, (4) spells "against slanderers and thieves," and (5) spells "against economic competitors."[46] In arranging his compendium of translated κατάδεσμοι, Gager follows a similar paradigm, although he adds one category for curses specifically relating to athletic competitions, another for "antidotes and counterspells," and a final all-encompassing miscellany to tie up loose ends which do not quite "fit" into any of the primary categories.[47] Although it is the amatory category with which subsequent analysis will be principally concerned, such groupings provide a useful frame within which to view binding activity.

2.2.2 Classification by *Modus Operandi*

More important to this study than the desired *ends* of binding curses are the *means* by which these curses were enacted and believed to operate. Faraone, building on Eugen G. Kagarow's classificatory model,[48] divides the *modi operandi* of the κατάδεσμοι into four categories.[49] The parameters of these groupings are largely defined by the verb forms used in the tablets, which greatly inform us as to the implicit assumptions made by the spell casters as to how their curses were thought to operate.

2.2.2.1 Unmediated Operations

The first category is made up of those direct binding spells denoted by first-person singular verbs which establish a direct operative link between the spell caster and his intended victim. A characteristic example of this can be seen in a fourth century BC tablet found in Attica whose function is to restrain a business competitor. One by one, the tablet's author names off local business operators whom he wishes to constrain from competing with him: "καταδῶ Καλλίαν" (I bind Kallias), "καταδῶ Σωσιμένεν" (I bind Sosimenes), "καταδῶ Κίττον" (I bind Kittos), "καταδῶ

---

[46]Graf, *Magic in the Ancient World*, 120–21.
[47]Gager, *Curse Tablets and Binding Spells from the Ancient World*, ix.
[48]Kagarow, *Griechische Fluchtafeln*, 28–34.
[49]Faraone, "The Agonistic Context of Early Greek Binding Spells," 5–10. Gager, ("Introduction," 13–14) adopts Faraone's model as well.

2.2. THEORY AND PRACTICE

Μανίαν" (I bind Mania), "τούτους πάντας καταδῶ" (I bind all of these).[50] As there is, in this instance, no *explicitly* noted intermediary bridging the "gap" between the operator and his victim, this type of κατάδεσμος appears to be either operating under the implicit assumption that the explicitly detailed means of the second, third, and fourth categories underlies his declaration.

2.2.2.2 Supernatural Mediation

The second category is composed of κατάδεσμοι which operate by means of the intercession of a supernatural intermediary enacting the operator's will upon his victim. Curiously, "notions of supplication or vow are absent or extremely rare in the *defixiones*."[51] Rather, the words addressed to the gods, daemons, or untimely dead in these tablets are generally phrased in the second-person imperative — *commanding* rather than petitioning the third party. A characteristic example of this type of coactive κατάδεσμος can be seen in a third or second century BC Attic tablet where the operator commands Hermes to bind several targets: "Ἑρμῆ χθόνιε ταῦτα οὕτω κάτεχε" (Chthonic Hermes, so bind them).[52] Regarding this implied divine coercion, H.S. Versnel notes that these modes of interaction with the gods tend to be more strongly represented among the older κατάδεσμοι, and that it is not until later periods that the relationship between the γόης and the gods is at times portrayed as supplicatory rather than manipulative.[53]

This inclusion of differing relational ideas is reflected in the language of the κατάδεσμοι. It is in this vein that Gager mentions that a brand of terminological legalism, "whereby the case of the target was handed over or transferred to divine jurisdiction," begins to emerge.[54] The regular verb in this instance is καταγράφω (I register),[55] and is used in the sense of dedicating the fate of the victim unto the god's jurisdiction. It is functionally identical

---

[50]*DTA*, 87a.
[51]Versnel, "Beyond Cursing," 61.
[52]*DT*, 52.14–16.
[53]Versnel, "Beyond Cursing," 93.
[54]Gager, "Introduction," 20.
[55]Faraone, "The Agonistic Context of Early Greek Binding Spells," 9; Graf, *Magic in the Ancient World*, 125–26.

with the καταδέω form, but represents an interpretative shift towards a more judicially minded view of the cursing process. An example of this can be seen in a tablet from Delos which dates from between the first century BC and the first century AD, where each body part of the victim is successively registered into the name and jurisdiction of the deities Suconaioi and Syria.[56] This method, wherein the individual body parts are named and dedicated to a god or gods, is, according to Graf, an adaption of a "well-known ritual of healing" from ancient Egyptian religion.[57]

2.2.2.3 Wish Formulae and *Similia Similibus*

Regarding his third and fourth categories, Faraone notes what while they may be "distinguished on formal grounds," they are often employed together.[58] Technically, the third category is the "wish formula," and is generally employed in tandem with the fourth, "*similia similibus* formula."[59] Treating them as one, this final category manifests itself as a wish for the victim to take on certain traits associated with something else — generally a component of the κατάδεσμος or an item located where the tablet was being deposited. For instance, one κατάδεσμος proclaims that the "ῥήματα" (spoken words) of Crates might be as "ψυχρὰ" (cold) and "ἐπαρίστερα" (from right to left, backwards) as those of the lead tablet upon which the curse was inscribed.[60] Faraone explains the theoretical underpinning of this type of κατάδεσμος not by an appellation to Frazer's notions of sympathetic and homeopathic magic, but rather by invoking Stanley Jeyaraja Tambiah's idea of persuasive analogy.[61] In this tablet's context, then, we could say that the γόης is not operating under assumptions rooted in a poor understanding of empirically observable cause and effect, but is rather working within a framework in which the

---

[56] *Curse Tablets and Binding Spells from the Ancient World*, 88a–b.

[57] Graf, *Magic in the Ancient World*, 144. For a detailed treatment of these rituals, dubbed *Gliedervergottung* by generations of German Egyptologists, see: Nyord, *Breathing Flesh*.

[58] Faraone, "The Agonistic Context of Early Greek Binding Spells," 6.

[59] Ibid.

[60] *DTA*, 67.

[61] Faraone, "The Agonistic Context of Early Greek Binding Spells," 8; Tambiah, "Form and Meaning of Magical Acts," 199–229.

"cold" and "backward" character of the κατάδεσμος will persuade the victim to take on those characteristics.

2.3 Gods, Daemons, and Ghosts

2.3.1 Theology of the Curse Tablets

Within the greater context of analysing θεαγωγία, two of the most important aspects of the κατάδεσμοι are the explicit ways in which the supernatural beings are petitioned, the specific beings — and types of beings — called upon, and the implicit presuppositions demonstrated by the language used. An understanding of how such beings "fit" into the world of the κατάδεσμοι is wholly necessary to frame the subsequent chapter on erotic ἀγωγή and ψυχαγωγία. The principal gods named in the κατάδεσμοι are generally chthonic and hold dominion over the underworld, death, and the ἀγωγή family of spells.[62] The most common Hellenic deities listed in the curse tablets include Hermes, Kore, Persephone, Hecate, Hades, Pluto, Gaia, and Demeter.[63] As the practice of crafting κατάδεσμοι perdured into the Hellenistic period, the types of intermediary beings involved tended to increase.[64] This list is expanded to include foreign gods such as the Brythonic Sulis, the Egyptian Osiris, and near Eastern gods such as the Gnostic god Iao and the Sumerian goddess Ereshkigal;[65] daemons both named individually (as strings of *nomina barbara*) and collectively, as with the Erinyes and various classes of nymphs;

---

[62] Versnel, "Beyond Cursing," 64. For more on the chthonic genus of gods, see: Fairbanks, "The Chthonic Gods of Greek Religion," 241–259.

[63] Kagarow, *Griehische Fluchtafeln*, 59–61; Versnel, "Beyond Cursing," 64; Faraone, "The Agonistic Context of Early Greek Binding Spells," 6; Gager, "Introduction," 12–13.

[64] Versnel, "Beyond Cursing," 61.

[65] Of all the deities present in the κατάδεσμοι, Ereshkigal is initially the most puzzling, due to the historical gap between her Sumerian cult in 3000 BC and the second to fifth century AD Hellenistic curse tablets. Despite the fact of the Sumerian civilization's decline and fall around 1900 BC, the continued usage of Sumerian as a liturgical and scribal language throughout the near East is widely responsible for such syncretic inclusions. For later uses of the Sumerian language in the Near East, see: Woodard, "Introduction," 9–11; Rubio, "The Invention of Sumerian," 247.

as well as the souls of the dead, both in the forms of the Roman Manes as well as the Hellenic ἄωροι (untimely dead).[66]

2.3.2 Daemonic Intermediaries

2.3.2.1 Origins in the Epic Period

There are several aspects of this intersection between the positions of the gods, daemons, and untimely dead in curse tablets that bear mention at this point. First, although philosophers from the Middle Platonic period onward were wont to make clear distinctions between the daemons and other classes of supernatural beings, this type of strict classification was significantly less clear among the γόητες and μάγοι who crafted the κατάδεσμοι.[67] While the term δαίμων (daemon) is "thoroughly Greek-looking," its etymological origin remains unclear.[68]

The senses conveyed by the attestations from the early Epic period range from that of a god to an "indefinite and not clearly personalised divine power" which is not quite a god, but is clearly supernatural.[69] The clearest characterisation of the δαίμονες of this period is one of classificatory indeterminacy.[70] For instance, in Homer's *Ilias* (eighth century BC), the army of gods gathered upon Olympus is collectively referred to as "δαίμονας."[71] Furthermore, later in the same poem, Helen is compared to Aphrodite, who is identified as a " δαίμων."[72] While this identification between the δαίμονες and the θεοί (gods) is somewhat clear in Homer, Hesiod's (seventh to eighth century BC) *Opera et dies* describes dead men of the Golden Age as "δαίμονες" — a "ἐσθλοί" (class) of beings which are "ἀλεξίκακοι" (deliverers from illness) and the "φύλακες" (guardians) of mankind.[73]

---

[66] Gager, "Introduction," 12–13; Jordan, "A Survey of Greek *Defixiones* Not Included in the Special Corpora," 152; Versnel, "Beyond Cursing," 64.
[67] Gager, "Introduction," 12.
[68] Burkert, *Greek Religion*, 180.
[69] Bassett, "ΔΑΙΜΩΝ in Homer," 134.
[70] Burkert, *Greek Religion*, 180.
[71] Homer, *The Iliad*, I.222.
[72] Homer, *The Iliad*, III.420.
[73] Hesiod, *Works and Days*, 122–23.

2.3.2.2 Platonic Transformations

Following in the wake of this loose and unsystemised use of the daemonic designation in the Epic period, Plato's *Symposium* presents the first philosophical model outlining the cosmological position and function of the δαίμονες. Therein, he describes them as being "μεταξύ ἐστι θεοῦ τε καὶ θνητοῦ" (in the midst of the divine and mortality) — conveying messages from the gods to men, and sacrifices from man to the gods.[74] Through Diomata's speech, then, Plato presents a cosmology in which the universe is plenary in nature, with the gods above, man below, and the medial zone occupied by daemons.[75]

Following this, as we progress into the Middle Platonic period, Plato's category is interpreted into two broad categories of theories exemplified by Xenocrates (c. 396 BC–c. 314) and Plutarch (AD 46–120) respectively.[76] The Xenocratean theory interprets daemonic nature in geometric terms. By means of an analogy, he describes the gods as equilateral triangles whose sides are all equal, mankind as scalene triangles whose sides are *all* unequal, and the mediating daemons as isosceles triangles which have partly equal and partly unequal sides. From this analogy, Xenocrates draws the conclusion that the δαίμονες mediate between the divine and human spheres of activity, and are in possession of both "πάθος θνητοῦ καὶ θεοῦ δύναμιν" (mortal passion and divine power).[77]

The contrary position develops out of Hesiod and Empedocles (c. 490–430 BC) — to whom Plutarch directly appeals. He notes Plato's description of the daemons as being an intermediary class of supernatural beings existing between gods and men, and weds this to both Hesiod's notion of "ἀγνοὺς δαίμονας" (good daemons) who are the "φύλακας ἀνθρώπων" (guardians of mankind) and Empedocles' idea of the δαίμονες as being the souls of dead men who are in the midst of becoming "κολασθέντες" (cleansed)

---

[74] Plato, *Symposium*, 202e.

[75] For more on these structural elements of Plato's cosmology in *Timaeus*, see: Cornford, *Plato's Cosmology*, 137–50; Mohr, *The Platonic Cosmology*, 171–77; Broadie, *Nature and Divinity in Plato's Timaeus*, 60–83.

[76] Dillon, *The Middle Platonists*, 46–47.

[77] Plutarch, *De defectu oraculorum*, 416c–d.

and "καθαρθέντες" (chastised) so as to achieve a higher, natural, position in the hierarchy of beings.[78]

2.3.2.3 Hecate, Daemons, and the Dead

The connection between the daemons and the souls of the dead is further exemplified by means of the goddess Hecate, in her guises as the queen both of daemons and the dead.[79] Hecate's position in relation to the daemons is revealed most clearly by Eusebius. In *Praeparatio evangelica*, he twice describes her as the ἄρχων (ruler) of the "πονηρῶν δαιμόνων" (malicious daemons).[80] As ruler of the dead, Hecate is described in Apollonius of Rhodes' (third century BC) *Argonautica* both as "χθονίην" (chthonic) and as the "ἐνέροισιν ἄνασσαν" (queen of those below), denoting her rulership over the dead.[81] This connection is strengthened by a passage from the *Orphici hymni* describing Hecate in connection with "ψυχαῖς νεκύων" (souls of the dead).[82]

The connection between the mistress of the daemons and the dead is drawn by linking Hecate with Selene, the goddess of the Moon.[83] In the earliest attestations, Hecate is associated directly with various liminal places, such as crossroads and doorways.[84] Examples of this can be seen in Sophocles (c. 497–406 BC), where "εἰνοδίας Ἑκάτης" (Hecate of the crossroads) is invoked[85] and in Aristophanes (c. 446–c. 386 BC), where he describes altars dedicated to Hecate "πανταχοῦ πρὸ τῶν θυρῶν" (before every doorway) in Athens.[86] Later, this idea of liminality was expanded to encompass the Moon, which was thought by many Middle Platonists to be a transmissive intermediary operating between the material Earth and intelligible Sun.[87] Within this Middle

---

[78] Plutarch, *De Iside et Osiride*, 361b–c.

[79] Johnston, *Hekate Soteira*, 33–35.

[80] Eusebius, *Eusebius Werke VIII*, III.16.2, IV.23.6. For a full exploration of the archontic classes, see: Plaisance, "Of Cosmocrators and Cosmic Gods," 64–85.

[81] Apollonius of Rhodes, *Apollonii Rhodii Argonautica*, 3.840.

[82] *Orphei hymni*, 1.3.

[83] Eusebius, *Eusebius Werke VIII*, III.16.2.

[84] Johnston, *Hekate Soteira*, 21–8.

[85] Sophocles, *Fragmenta*, fr. 535.2.

[86] Aristophanes, *Vespae*, 804.

[87] Johnston, *Hekate Soteira*, 29.

2.3. GODS, DAEMONS, AND GHOSTS

Figure 2.1: A Roman marble copy of a Hellenistic original statue depicting Hecate's triple-formed representation, from the Museo Chiaramonti's collection (Inv. 1922). Photo by Jastrow, 2006.

Platonic milieu, the Moon was also associated both with daemons and the souls of the dead[88] — a role filled by terrestrial liminal locales as well.[89]

2.3.2.4 Intermediary Nexus

This network of connections between the gods, daemons, and souls of the dead within the context of the καταδεσμοι, is further cemented by the deep link between the γόης and the practice of ψυχαγωγία. As mentioned previously, the characteristic activity of the γόης — γοητεία — derives from the term γόος, an archaic term for the funerary lament. This etymological tie between the archaic wailing hymns to the dead of early antiquity and γοητεία helps us establish an initial link between γοητεία and ψυχαγωγία.[90] Apart from the origin of the word itself, there are two key literary examples which clearly illustrate the point.

The first is the previously cited entry from the *Suda*, wherein γοητεία is defined as "ἀνάγειν νεκρὸν" (evocation of the dead).[91] Second, Plato's *Leges* makes a similar identification, describing ψυχαγωγία as being accomplished by means of "ἐπῳδαῖς γοητεύοντες" (beguiling spells).[92] And while the *Suda* clearly distinguishes between the γόης and μάγος, earlier texts, such as the *Papyrus Derveni*, grant the μάγος the ability to control the "δαίμονας ἐμποδὼν" (obstructing daemons) — daemons who are identified as "ψυχαῖς ἐχθροί" (hateful souls).[93] In this, then, we see the evidence of the distinct likelihood that both the γόης and the μάγος were seen as practitioners of ψυχαγωγία, and that this practice was intimately bound up both with invocations of the gods that bordered on being (if not overtly) compulsory and the construction of καταδεσμοι.

---

[88] Johnston, *Hekate Soteira*, 35–36.
[89] Johnston, *Restless Dead*, 171; Johnston, "Crossroads," 223-4.
[90] Johnston, *Restless Dead*, 102–03; Collins, *Magic in the Ancient Greek World*, 58–59.
[91] *Sudiae lexicon*, s.v. "γοητεία."
[92] Plato, *Leges*, 909b.
[93] *The Derveni Papyrus*, VI.2–4.

2.3.3 Case Study (*PGM* XV)

2.3.3.1 Ritual Mechanics

This unity of this broad constellation of concepts can be best illustrated by means of a concrete instance from the *PGM* which incorporates nearly everything described thus far in this subchapter within the context of a single κατάδεσμος spell. This spell, *PGM* XV, is untitled in the manuscript, but is clearly a κατάδεσμος of the erotic variety. Karl Preisendanz locates the papyrus in the Musée gréco-romain d'Alexandrie,[94] and it has been dated as being third century AD by Betz.[95] The spell announces its intention thusly, with the γόης saying to his intended victim: "ἵνα καταδήσωσι Νῖλον" (I will bind you, Nilos).[96] Her curse compels Nilos to love her — or her client — completely, such that she deserts her parents, children, and friends.[97] This curse — which the γόης claims that "οὐδὲ θεῶν οὐδὲ ἀνθρώπων" (neither god nor man) will break[98] — is enforced not by one of the groups discussed above, but by all of them.

To bind Nilos, she calls on the souls of the "ἄπαιδας" (childless) and "ἀγάμους" (unmarried) dead;[99] the various "δαίμονες, τοὺς ἐν τῷ τόπῳ" (daemons who are in this place);[100] various "daemons" who are clearly identifiable as non-Hellenic gods, such as Iao and Sabaoth;[101] and even "ἐν τῷ οὐρανῷ θεὸς ὁ μονογενές" (the sole god in heaven).[102] The intercession of the gods, daemons and ghosts are effected by means of the verbs "ἐξορκίζω" (I conjure),[103] "ὁρκίζω" (I adjure),[104] and "διορκίζω" (I adjure)[105]

---

[94] Preisendanz (ed.), *PGM*, 2:133.
[95] Betz, "List of Papyri in Preisendanz," xxiii.
[96] *PGM*, XV.1.
[97] Ibid., XV.4–5.
[98] Ibid., XV.2.
[99] Ibid., XV.8.
[100] Ibid., XV.5.
[101] Ibid., XV.15. Iao and Sabaoth are two of the hebdomadic archons listed throughout *Nag Hammadi* codices. For more on this theological structure, see: van den Broek, "The Creation of Adam's Psychic Body in the Apocryphon of John," 38–57.
[102] Ibid., XV.16.
[103] Ibid., XV.5.
[104] Ibid., XV.10.
[105] Ibid., XV.13.

all of which clearly places the γόης in the position of exerting compulsory authority over these various classes of supernatural beings so that they might bind her victim, Nilos.

2.3.3.2 Connections to Θεαγωγία

In summation, this binding spell from *PGM* XV serves to exemplify nearly everything that has been discussed regarding κατάδεσμοι and the operative technology used by the γόητες thus far. For, in this spell, we see the γόης bind her victim by compelling a host of gods, daemons, and dead souls — all actions which we have seen to be the characteristic activities and techniques associated both with γοητεία and the κατάδεσμοι. Furthermore, by exemplifying the compulsory nature of the relationship between the γόης and the supernatural beings upon which he calls, this spell serves both as a direct link between the curse tablets and the ἀγωγή family of spells to be discussed in the following chapter and the specific subject of θεαγωγία with which we are principally concerned here.

In connection to the practice of θεαγωγία, the κατάδεσμοι have shown themselves to be important objects of inquiry not because they resemble the rituals of divine evocation, but rather because the means by which they effect their intended bindings often make use of ritual formulae whereby the γόης or μάγος compels the gods to do his bidding. This concept, that the gods can be forced into the performance of specified actions by an operator is key to understanding both the θεαγωγία itself as a practice and the greater "magical" context within which it was viewed at the time. And, the fact that this methodology of coercion — divine or otherwise — is so completely and utterly pervasive within the Graeco-Roman curse tablets, makes it an intrinsically necessary inclusion in our attempt to understand what θεαγωγία meant to the late antique practitioner.

Chapter 3

Erotic Enchantments

3.1 Origins of Ἀγωγή

3.1.1 Foundational Classifications

For the purposes of investigating θεαγωγία, the most important stream to flow from the κατάδεσμοι is the ἀγωγή family of spells. This category of spell is defined by the intent to lead an intended subject toward the spell caster.[1] Faraone traces the origin of the term ἀγωγή to the verb ἄγειν,[2] meaning "to lead, fetch, or bring."[3] Although the act of bringing may, at first, seem disconnected from the act of binding previously discussed in terms of the κατάδεσμοι, we shall see presently how the latter flows naturally into the former both in terms of intent and ritual morphology.

The primary repository of these ἀγωγή spells is the *PGM*, wherein they come in three varieties which will be examined in turn: (1) the erotic class, designed to lead a living person to the evocator; (2) the necromantic class, designed to lead the soul of a dead person to the evocator; and (3) the divine class, designed to lead daemons and gods to the evocator. This present chapter will examine the historical origins and textual instantiations of the first class, specifically focusing on their formative relationship

---

[1] Faraone, *Ancient Greek Love Magic*, 25–26; Collins, *Magic in the Ancient Greek World*, 88.

[2] Faraone, *Ancient Greek Love Magic*, 25.

[3] *LSJ*, s.v. "ἄγω."

with the third category within which θεαγωγία is classed.

3.1.2 Early Examples

3.1.2.1 Sappho

The term ἀγωγή is so strongly linked to the first class of erotic spells that both ancient[4] and modern[5] sources use it — bereft of any modifiers — to specifically refer to this type of operation. In this context, the term is most often used to designate rituals designed to lead a woman from her home, into the arms of the γόης or — more often — his client.[6] Although Faraone identifies the first instance of a ritual rubric being titled "'Αγωγή" in the third century AD papyrus,[7] he traces its origin to the hymns of the ancient lyric poets Sappho (fifth century BC) and Pindar (c. 522–443 BC).[8] In one of Sappho's hymns to Aphrodite, she has the goddess query why she is to "πείθω" (persuade) and "ἄγεν" (lead) Sappho's lover back into her arms.[9] Interestingly, the use of the term πείθω in this fragment has the additional subtextual connotation of Πείθω as not only being a Greek verb, but also a minor Goddess — a handmaiden of Aphrodite seen as embodying persuasion and seduction.[10]

In any event, the implication which Faraone draws from Sappho's use of this terminology of leading and persuasion is that her prior prayers to Aphrodite to which this speech was a response were a type of ἀγωγή spell intended to draw her intended lover to her.[11] While this literary example does not clearly indicate a ritual component, Sappho's use of terminology specifically linked with spells of erotic compulsion within the context of a petition to Aphrodite at the very least seems to indicate some connection between such rituals and the term ἀγωγή.

---

[4] For two characteristic examples, see: *PGM*, IV.1390–1495, VII.593–619.

[5] Winkler, "The Constraints of Eros," 215–6; Faraone, *Ancient Greek Love Magic*, 25–26.

[6] Ibid., 56.

[7] Faraone, *Ancient Greek Love Magic*, 26. Here, he is referencing *PGM*, LXI.39–44.

[8] Faraone, *Ancient Greek Love Magic*, 56.

[9] Sappho, *Sappho*, fr. 1.18–9.

[10] Buxton, *Persuasion in Greek Tragedy*, 31–47

[11] Faraone, *Ancient Greek Love Magic*, 136.

3.1.2.2 Pindar

The second ancient example Faraone notes is from Pindar's *Pythia*, where — while relaying the tale of Jason and Medea — he tells of the "λιτάς τ' ἐπαοιδὰς" (prayer spells) taught to Jason by Aphrodite herself.[12] Faraone's exegesis of this passage draws a tentative connection to the later ἀγωγή spells by means of etymological analysis.[13] The term λιτή (pl. λιτάς) generally means "prayer," and has the specific connotation of being an entreaty to the gods.[14] The term itself is derived from the verb λίτομαι, or λίσσομαι, meaning "to beg" or "to pray"[15] — indicating that this hymn is petitionary in nature, and participates in a relationship between Jason and Aphrodite. The second term, ἐπαοιδή or ἐπῳδή, has the specific connotation of being an incantation directed against another target.[16] This is owed, according to Faraone,[17] to the fact that the word is a compound of ἀοιδή, meaning "song" and often having the sense of an incantation,[18] and ἐπί, which, in its "hostile sense," means "against." [19]

Thus, we are presented with an example wherein Aphrodite teaches Jason a hymnic incantation which is to be used against Medea. The intended result of this ἐπαοιδή exemplifies two themes we shall see repeated throughout the later history of the erotic ἀγωγή spell as well. The spell specifically indicates that Medea will be robbed of reverence for her parents ("τοκέων ἀφέλοιτ' αἰδῶ") such that she will leave the family home and flee into Jason's arms.[20] This culturally heterodox behavior is to be effected by the μάστιξ (whip, or scourge) of the goddess Peitho[21] — which hearkens strongly back to the dual sense of "persuasion" as both a coactive force within the context of a spell as well as a goddess that we previously saw in the example from Sappho.

---

[12]Pindar, *The Pythian Odes*, IV.213–19.
[13]Faraone, *Ancient Greek Love Magic*, 137.
[14]*LSJ*, s.v. "λιτή."
[15]Ibid., s.v. "λίτομαι," s.v. "λίσσομαι."
[16]Ibid., s.v. "ἐπαοιδή," s.v. "ἐπῳδή."
[17]Faraone, *Ancient Greek Love Magic*, 137.
[18]*LSJ*, s.v. "ἀοιδή."
[19]Ibid., s.v. "ἐπί."
[20]Pindar, *The Pythian Odes*, IV.218.
[21]Ibid., IV.219.

3.1.3 Connections to Bridal Theft Traditions

3.1.3.1 Mythological Roots

These two points raised in Pindar's ode — the theme of the female victim being taken from her family home and the violent imagery associated with the ἀγωγή spell's operative mechanism — are important in that they are highly suggestive as to the origins of the ἀγωγαί. The first point can be, according to Faraone, used to help demonstrate direct parallels between erotic ἀγωγή spells and the form of marriage which was common throughout the Mediterranean commonly referred to as bridal theft.[22] As a means by which a bride was acquired by a prospective suitor, the practice is well attested throughout antique literature. From a mythological angle, we see a clear instance in the story of Persephone.

Hesiod describes her as having been "ἥρπασε ἧς παρὰ μητρός" (snatched away from her mother), Demeter, by the King Aïdoneus, to whom she was then wed.[23] The alternative version of this story, where Persephone tells Demeter of having been "βῆ δὲ φέρων ὑπὸ γαῖαν" (carried away underground) by her future husband Hades, is found in the *Hymni Homerici*.[24] One of the clearest examples of large-scale bridal theft, or more properly *rapito* in this instance, is the story of the rape of the Sabine women — relayed in Livy's (59 BC–AD 17) *Ab urbe condita libri* — whereupon in 752 BC the armies of the legendary Roman founder Romulus were said to have abducted *en masse* the women of the Sabine tribe with whom the fledgling Romans were then at war.[25] Contrary to modern connotations of the word "rape," this instance of *rapito* did not necessarily entail a sexual assault on the battle field; rather, the women were pressed into marrying Roman men.

---

[22] Faraone, *Ancient Greek Love Magic*, 78–94.
[23] Hesiod, *The Theogony*, 913–14.
[24] *The Homeric Hymns*, II.431.
[25] Livy, *History of Rome*, I.9–13.

3.1.3.2 Historical Traditions

Judith Evans-Grubbs provides perhaps the clearest presentation of the practice of bridal theft in the Graeco-Roman world by means of a sociological exegesis of Emperor Constantine's (AD c. 272–337) law against it.[26] Preserved in the *Codex Theodosianus* of Emperor Theodosius II (AD 401–450), the law makes it illegal for a man to either seize an unwilling girl or lead a willing girl from her parents' custody without having made a prior arrangement with them.[27] Evans-Grubbs describes the practice illegalised by Constantine as "the abduction of an unmarried girl by an man who has not made a formal betrothal agreement with her but who hopes to force her parents' consent to what is essentially a *de facto* marriage."[28]

As Faraone notes, the "crucial difference between" bridal theft and contractual marriages is "the public consent or willingness of the bride."[29] This is to say that in antiquity, it was not uncommon for bridal abduction to function as a face-saving ritual. In such instances — say, where a child was conceived out of wedlock, or where the prospective groom could not afford the appropriate dowry — the "theft" of the bride allows all parties to achieve reasonable satisfaction through the maintenance of a fictive cover story.

3.1.3.3 Erotic Spells and Bridal Theft

The connection between these real and fictive bridal abductions and the verbiage in the ἀγωγαί is such that the prevalence of such marriage in Graeco-Roman culture and literature appears to have served as an influencing factor in the often violent imagery in the ἀγωγή spells. Faraone notes two broad similarities that serve to connect: (1) that both techniques of acquiring a woman utilize violence, and (2) that in each case the violence is temporary.[30] First is the violent treatment of the woman who is the intended victim of the γόης. A prime example of this type of operation

---

[26] Evans-Grubbs, "Abduction Marriage in Antiquity," 59–83.
[27] Theodosius II, *Theodosiani libri XVI*, IX.24.1.
[28] Evans-Grubbs, "Abduction Marriage," 61.
[29] Faraone, *Ancient Greek Love Magic*, 79.
[30] Faraone, *Ancient Greek Love Magic*, 86–87, 93–94.

in action is the spell titled, "Ἀγωγὴ ἐπί ζμύρνης ἐπιθυομένης" (Evocation Wherein Myrrh is Sacrificed), from the Paris magical papyrus.[31] Therein, the γόης announces the spell's intended goal as having the myrrh — which is itself later identified with a whole host of identifiable god-names and *nomina barbara* — "ἵνα μοι ἄξῃς αὐτήν" (lead [the girl against whom the spell is directed] here to me).[32]

While this goal seems fairly reasonable for a love spell, the means by which he intends to effect it appears rather disjunctive to modern readers. He begins by instructing the myrrh to deprive her of the pleasures of common daily activities, such as: sitting, conversing, meeting with friends, walking about, drinking, eating, kissing, and sleeping.[33] This deprivation of pleasure presumably not being sufficient to compel the girl to come to the γόης, the myrrh is instructed to "ἔμμεινον" (abide in) and "καῦσον" (kindle, or burn) various parts of the girl's anatomy "ἕως ἔλθῃ πρὸς ἐμέ" (until she comes unto me).[34] The ritual mechanism is familiar to us from the analogical κατάδεσμοι, with the γόης inducing the figurative "burning" within his female victim by means literally burning the myrrh within a fire.[35] This technique used in this spell, thus, highlights the "close formal affinities" both between the ἀγωγή spells and κατάδεσμοι, and between ἀγωγαί and the violence associated with abduction marriage.[36]

The torments directed against the girls who are the intended victims of such violent ἀγωγαί are, however, strictly incidental to the spells and are of a strictly limited duration. In the above spell from *PGM* IV.1496–1595, we see this stated quite clearly. For, while the γόης does incite the myrrh to inflict all manners of violence upon the girl; they are clearly stated to take place only until she comes to him — to "φιλοῦσά με καὶ ποιήσῃ πάντα τὰ

---

[31] *PGM*, IV.1496–1595. E.N. O'Neil, in his translation of this spell in Betz' *GMPT*, translates the title as: "Love spell of attraction over myrrh which is offered."

[32] *PGM*, IV.1509–10. Here, we see the operative verb as "ἄξῃς," which is a rarely attested form of ἄγω.

[33] Ibid., IV.1510–22.

[34] Ibid., IV.1527–31.

[35] Ibid., IV.1541ff.

[36] Faraone, *Ancient Greek Love Magic*, 80.

θελήματά μου" (love me and fulfill all of my desires).[37] This chain of events, where torments are temporarily visited upon a female victim until she is driven into the "loving" arms of the γόης, are not limited to this particular spell, but are rather common throughout the ἀγωγή genre.[38]

Faraone compares this process of "initial violence" that leads to "a settled and even happy relationship" to the bridal abduction, noting that such social processes "are clearly part of a traditional [...] pattern of thought that viewed the bride-to-be as a member of a hostile tribe of sorts who had to be violently raped — in both its original meaning of 'kidnapped' and its later connotations of sexual penetration — to ensure that she sever her loyalty to her natal family and irrevocably cast her lot with her new husband."[39] This is to say that, as in the case of bridal theft, the violence with which the ἀγωγαί operate is not the end of the spell, but is rather the means through which the end must necessarily be obtained. Outside the confines of a legally sanctioned betrothal contract, the only way for a man to gain a woman was through force. And, as we have seen, such force could be conveyed by conventional physical means or by the less conventional techniques of the γόης.

3.2 Ἀγωγαί and Κατάδεσμοι

3.2.1 Connective Matrix

While the previous section has demonstrated continuities between the erotic ἀγωγή spells and both the traditions of hymnic poetry and bridal abduction, there is one further connection to be made: that between the ἀγωγή spells and the curse tablets discussed in the second chapter. For the purposes of our examination of the historical origins of θεαγωγία, this connection is of particular importance. For, if a lineage can be established from the curse tablets, to the erotic spells, to the theagogic evocations, then philosophical reactions to θεαγωγία — such as those

---

[37] *PGM*, IV.1531–3.
[38] For illustrative examples, see: *PGM*, IV.296–466; IV.2441–2621; IV.2708–84.
[39] Faraone, *Ancient Greek Love Magic*, 94.

of Iamblichus — can be contextualised within the broader context of the negative opinions of the κατάδεσμοι in particular and of γοητεία in general by the intellectuals in Greece and Rome.

The connection between the ἀγωγαί and the κατάδεσμοι is noted by Faraone,[40] Gager,[41] and Ogden[42] — with the latter two treating the ἀγωγή as a sub-category of κατάδεσμος. The key operative difference between the two categories appears to be that the early curse tablets which we can identify as κατάδεσμοι as opposed to being ἀγωγαί are concerned with enacting retributive violence against the women with which they are concerned rather than the kind of "purposeful" violence that *leads* the women towards the γόητες. An early example of this type can be seen in a folded lead tablet from Attica, which seeks to "καταδοῦμεν" (bind) the genitals of a rival's household.[43] However, by the time we reach the Hellenistic period, the foci of erotic binding spells was more explicitly to utilise binding and force to bring the woman to the γόης.

3.2.2 Case Study A (The Sword of Dardanos)

According to Winkler, there are two spells among the magical papyri whose verbiage best illustrate the deep connection between the mechanics of the κατάδεσμοι and ἀγωγαί.[44] The first of these is the spell entitled, "Ξίφος Δαρδάνου" (The Sword of Dardanos),[45] whose primary function is to "κλίνει γὰρ καὶ ἄγει ψυχήν" (incline towards and fetch the soul) of an intended victim.[46] In his commentary on this spell, Betz notes that "since the operator does not want spiritual love, ψυχή here is probably the female pudenda."[47] The spell's central mechanism is an engraved "λίθον μάγνητα πνέοντα" (magnetic stone exuding

---

[40] Faraone, *Ancient Greek Love Magic*, 13–14, 30, 51, 62–63, 84, 143–44.
[41] Gager, "Sex, Love, and Marriage," 78–85.
[42] Ogden, *Magic, Witchcraft, and Ghosts in the Greek and Roman Worlds*, 227.
[43] *DTA*, 77.
[44] Winkler, "The Constraints of Eros," 231.
[45] *PGM*, IV.1716–1870.
[46] Ibid., IV.1721.
[47] *GMPT*, ff. 218

3.2. ΑΓΩΓΑΙ AND ΚΑΤΑΔΕΣΜΟΙ

breath/spirit)⁴⁸ displaying two images, one on each side.

In examining this operative mechanism, we should note that the key verb used here, πνέω, carries both the senses of exhaling literal breath and the vital spirit. The first side of the graven stone is of Psyche being ridden by Aphrodite — who is gripping the former's hair — while Eros burns Psyche from below with a torch.⁴⁹ On the opposite side is inscribed an image of Psyche and Eros in each other's arms.⁵⁰ The rubric instructs the γόης to place the stone under his tongue and intone a poetic hymn to Eros so as to activate the stone's powers.⁵¹ This image, of Psyche — who represents the "soul" of the woman who is the intended victim of the γόης — being tormented by Eros immediately calls to mind Pindar's previously discussed poem, where Medea is compelled into Jason's arms by Peitho's whip.⁵²

3.2.3 Case Study B (Φιλτροκατάδεσμος)

3.2.3.1 Etymological Questions

As extreme as such images of one's desired "lover" being scourged and immolated by deities of erotic furor might be, Winkler's second example takes the theme of erotic violence to another level entirely. This spell is titled "Φιλτροκατάδεσμος θαυμαστός,"⁵³ which is difficult to translate idiomatically. The first term is only attested in two other locations in the Greek corpus,⁵⁴ and is a compound word composed of two roots: φίλτρον (pl. φίλτρα) and the all too familiar κατάδεσμος. Φίλτρον is a term for spells meant to induce affection — itself deriving from φιλέω (to love) — that often bears the connotation of a potion.⁵⁵ Faraone's anal-

---

[48] *PGM*, IV.1722.

[49] Ibid., IV.1722–37.

[50] Ibid., IV.1737–43.

[51] Ibid., IV.1743–8. The hymn itself is taken from a separate spell: Ibid., IV.1748–1833.

[52] Pindar, *The Pythian Odes*, IV.218.

[53] *PGM*, IV.296–466.

[54] *LMPG*, s.v. "φιλτροκατάδεσμος." The first instance is *PGM*, VIII.1–63, which is a spell titled, "Φιλτροκατάδεσμος Ἀστραψοίχου." *SM* 38.8 is the second attestation. In this a binding spell with the γόης specifically identifies as a "φιλτροκαταδέσμου."

[55] *LSJ*, s.v. "φίλτρον."

ysis divides the ἀγωγαί and φίλτρα as being broadly differentiated categories of "love" spells.

Whereas the former tend to carry the specific intentions of inducing "uncontrollable lust" in their intended victims, the latter seek to kindle a more benign species of affection that is less overtly sexual in nature.[56] What is particularly interesting about the φιλτροκατάδεσμος compound, however, is that the combination of φίλτρον and κατάδεσμος is grouped with the ἀγωγαί spells rather than the φίλτρα potions.[57] The second term, θαυμαστός, simply means "wonderfull," or "marvelous."[58] This combines with φιλτροκατάδεσμος to allow us to interpret the title as referring to a highly effective spell designed to induce lust in its victim by means of binding — which is precisely what *PGM* IV.296–466 delivers.

3.2.3.2 Physical and Emotional Bondage

The "Φιλτροκατάδεσμος θαυμαστός," is one of the most picturesque examples of the intersection between the ἀγωγαί and κατάδεσμοι. At the beginning of the spell's invocation, the γόης specifically addresses the "θεοῖς χθονίοις" (chthonic gods), entrusting to them "τοῦτον τὸν κατάδςσμον" (this binding spell), whose purpose is to "ἄξον καὶ κατάδησον" (fetch and bind) the female object of his desire.[59] The spell caster clarifies his intent, imploring the chthonic gods and daemons at once to cause the victim to "φιλοῦσάν με" (love me) and to prevent her from obtaining "ἡδονὴν [...] μετ' ἄλλου ἀνδρός" (pleasure with another man).[60]

These binary foci culminate in the spell's final adjuration to the chthonic powers, with the γόης commanding them to "ἄξον" (fetch) and "κατάδησον" (bind) her so that she will be filled with "φιλοῦσαν" (affection), "ἐρῶσαν" (lust), and "ποθοῦσαν" (yearning) for him "εἰς τὸν ἄπαντα χρόνον τοῦ αἰῶνος" (throughout all time and eternity).[61] This stated purpose demonstrates well that

---

[56] Faraone, *Ancient Greek Love Magic*, 28–9.

[57] Ibid., *Ancient Greek Love Magic*, 28.

[58] *LSJ*, s.v. "θαυμαστος."

[59] *PGM*, IV.336–350. As with *PGM*, IV.1509–10, we see ἄξον here as an unusual form of ἄγω.

[60] *PGM*, IV.351–53.

[61] Ibid., IV.395–406.

the spell's author saw the activities of fetching and binding to be, if not identical, closely related. Additionally, it makes clear the purpose of the φιλτροκατάδεσμος to not only make the woman come to the γόης, but also to make her *feel* the emotions of a lover. This added layer of emotional compulsion is most readily explained by analysing the most famous component of the spell: its accompanying "voodoo" doll.

3.2.3.3 Paired Effigies

As Faraone notes, this "overlap between curses and erotic spells is [...] most dramatically illustrated in the use of paired effigies" within the context of this particular spell.⁶² The two statues described in the spell are to be crafted from either wax or clay, with one representing "Ἄρεα καθωπλισμένον" (Ares fully-armed) and the other being a female figure with "ὀπισθάγγωνα" (bound hands) who is "ἐπὶ τὰ γόνατα καθημένην" (seated on her knees) — while Ares stands "κρατοῦντα ξίφος" (mighty with a sword), prepared to stab the girl through the neck.⁶³ The figure of the female, who Faraone identifies as Aphrodite,⁶⁴ has every part of her body covered in *nomina barbara*.⁶⁵

These same parts of the figurine's body — her brain, ears, eyes, mouth, belly, hands, genitals, and feet — are then each pierced with one of thirteen copper needles (see Figure 3.1), while the γόης chants: "περονῶ τὸ ποιὸν μέλος τῆς δεῖνα, ὅπως μηδενὸς μνησθῇ πλὴν ἐμοῦ μόνου, τοῦ δεῖνα" ("I am piercing such and such member of her, NN, so that she may remember no one but me, NN, alone").⁶⁶ The statue was then to be wrapped in a lead sheet — recalling the uses of lead as the primary material component in the construction of curse tablets — upon which was inscribed the spell detailed in the previous paragraph. This was then deposited at the gravesite of "ἀώρου" (untimely) and "βιαίου" (violent) dead.⁶⁷ This statue's description impresses deeply

---

⁶²Faraone, *Ancient Greek Love Magic*, 51.

⁶³*PGM*, IV.296–303.

⁶⁴Faraone, *Ancient Greek Love Magic*, 52–53.

⁶⁵*PGM*, IV.304–21.

⁶⁶*PGM*, IV.321–30. The translation of the final passage is from O'Neil's translation of the spell in *GMPT*.

⁶⁷*PGM*, IV.332–4.

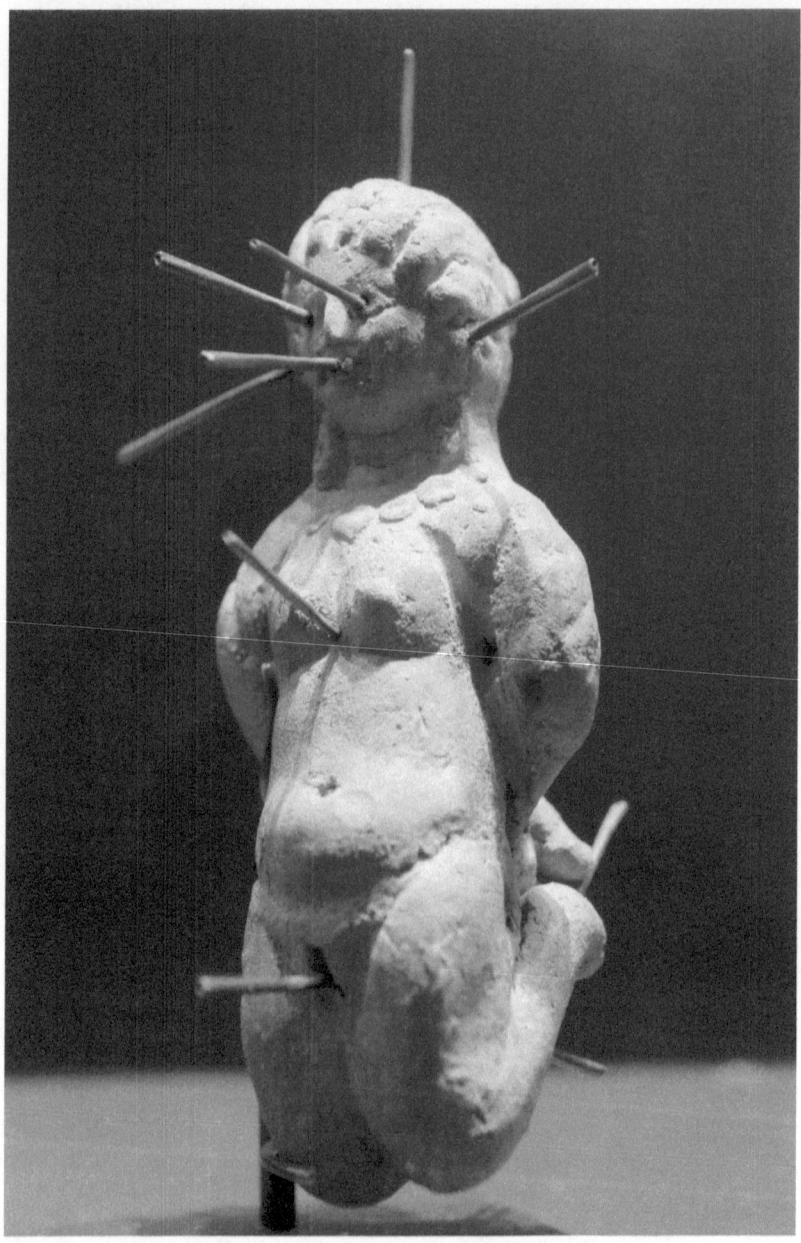

Figure 3.1: The effigy found paired with the papyrus on which *PGM* IV.296–466 is attested, currently in the Louvre Museum's collection (E 27145b). Photo by Marie-Lan Nguyen, 2014.

the core essence of the φιλτροκατάδεσμοι, that "the fundamental idea behind binding spells and *agōgai* alike is constraint."⁶⁸

3.3 Ἀνάγκη and Spells of Compulsion

3.3.1 Compulsion and Θεαγωγία

There is, in this spell, no suggestion that the component is separate from the ἀγωγή. Rather, the whole thrust of the spell is that it is through binding that compulsive fetching of the ἀγωγή is effected. Apart from an intimate connection between κατάδεσμοι and ἀγωγαί spells, what the above exegeses demonstrate is a thesis worked out in full by Heinz Schreckenberg, that ἀνάγκη (necessity) is the means through which ἀγωγή is made effective.⁶⁹ Schreckenberg's analysis of this relationship provides a key segue pertinent to our overarching theme of θεαγωγία, noting: "Die Formel, die den Gott herbeiführt, heiß auch θεαγωγὸς λόγος, denn die ἀνάγκη wird im ἄγειν wirksam" (The formula, which compels a god, is also called formula of divine evocation, since it is through necessity that compulsion becomes effective).⁷⁰

What is important to note about Schreckenberg's thesis is that, (1) he affirms the connection between θεαγωγία and ἀγωγή and (2) he positions ἀνάγκη as the operative core of both. Ἀνάγκη, as it is defined in the *LSJ*, principally translates as either "force, constraint, [or] necessity"; secondarily as "necessity in the philosophical sense" (i.e. either as necessary conditions or as fate); and thirdly as specifically referring to "compulsion exerted by a superior."⁷¹ While the philosophical sense of ἀνάγκη will be quite important for our foray into Iamblichus' discussion of the "θεῶν ἀνάγκαι" (necessities of the gods) in chapter five,⁷² it is the more general sense of forceful compulsion that applies at this juncture.

---

⁶⁸Winkler, "The Constraints of Eros," 231.
⁶⁹Schreckenberg, *Ananke*, 6–13, 135–64.
⁷⁰Ibid., 156.
⁷¹*LSJ*, s.v. "ἀνάγκη."
⁷²Iamblichus, *On the Mysteries*, I.14.

3.3.2 Ἀνάγκη in the *PGM*

Within the *PGM*, the most commonly encountered "magical" variant of ἀνάγκη is the term ἐπάναγκος (pl. ἐπάναγκοι), which the *LMPG* translates as "fórmula coactiva" (coercive formula).[73] Generally, such formulas are present in spells whose rubrics are formally identical to the ἀγωγή spells — and, indeed, the two spell categories demonstrate a high degree of overlap. *PGM* IV.2441–2621 demonstrates this perfectly. The spell's title is simply "Ἀγωγή," and its stated purpose is to "ἄγουσα" (fetch) a woman by "καταχλίνει" (striking with disease) and "ὀνειροπομπεῖ" (sending dreams).[74] These are, as we have seen, somewhat standard methods for an ἀγωγή spell to torture the intended victim of the γόης into coming to him.

What is interesting here is that the second part of the spell includes a postscript, instructing the reader to use the given hymn for ἐπαναγκαστικῶν,[75] a term derived from ἐπάναγκος which the *LMPG* translates as "fórmulas o prácticas coactivas" (coercive formulas or practices).[76] This is immediately followed by a third section, identified as an "ἐπάναγκος λόγος" (coercive spell),[77] which calls principally on a syncretised Selene Hecate to "ἄγε μοι τὴν δεῖνα τάχιστα" (swiftly bring her, NN, to me).[78] It is of interest that here, in this final line of the spell, that the author uses the *imperative* conjugation of ἄγω — effectively *commanding* the goddess to fetch him the girl.[79] While it was mentioned earlier that, within the context of the κατάδεσμοι, second-person imperative verbs *implicitly* imbued the spells with undertones of divine compulsion, it is with the ἐπάναγκοι that we finally begin to see this idea move from being implicit to explicit.

---

[73] LMPG, s.v. "ἐπάναγκος."
[74] *PGM*, IV.2441–44.
[75] Ibid., IV.2567–68.
[76] *LMPG*, s.v. "ἐπαναγκαστικός."
[77] *PGM*, IV.2573.
[78] Ibid., IV.2679–80.
[79] For more analysis of this spell, see: Pachoumi, *The Concept of the Divine in the Greek Magical Papyri*, 133–36.

3.3.3 Case Study (*PGM* IV.2891–2942)

3.3.3.1 Structure of the Spell

This nexus of ἀνάγκη and ἀγωγή, wherein the deity called upon is forcefully compelled to effect the fetching is best exemplified in ΠΓΜ IV.2891–2942, an "Ἀγωγή" spell whose key participants are the γόης, his intended victim, and the goddess Aphrodite. The spell's intent is typical of ἀγωγαί — to compel a woman to come to the spell caster — but the means through which this is effected is quite different from the spells we have examined previously. The spell consists of three sections: (1) "Πρὸς τὸν ἀστέρα τῆς Ἀφροδίτης ἐπίθυμα" (A Burned Offering to Aphrodite's Star),[80] (2) "Ἐπάναγκος τῆς πράξεως" (Ritual of Compulsion),[81] and (3) "Ἐπάναγκος" (Compulsive Spell).[82] The first section is of no particular interest here, as it strictly concerns the preparation of the offering which is to be burned in sacrifice to Aphrodite.

The second and third sections, however, are quite a different story. The second section begins by directly *threatening* Aphrodite, admonishing her that if she is not quick enough in fulfilling the will of the γόης, then she "οὐκ ὄψῃ τὸν Ἄδωνιν ἀνερχόμενον Ἀΐδαο" (will not see Adonis ascend from Hades),[83] for the γόης himself will "δήσω δεσμοῖς" (bind) Adonis.[84] The section of the spell continues with this obviously impious line of address, culminating with the γόης saying, "ὁρκίζω γάρ Κυθήρη" (I adjure you, Cytherea), and then doing so by means of a string of *nomina barbara*.[85] The third section begins in a more prosaic manner, with the mixture of hexameter verse interspersed with *voces magicae* that is characteristic of the *PGM*'s spells. However the final two lines of the hymn impel the "Κυπρογένεια θεά" (Cyprus-born goddess) to "τέλει τελέαν ἐπαοιδήν" (completely

---

[80]*PGM*, IV.2891–92.
[81]Ibid., IV.2901.
[82]Ibid., IV.2915.
[83]Ibid., IV.2903. This line is perhaps an allusion to *Orphei hymni* 56.8–11, wherein Adonis is described as dwelling below in Tartarus only to ultimately ascend upwards to Olympus.
[84]*PGM*, IV.2904.
[85]Ibid., IV.2912–14.

fulfill [this] incantation).⁸⁶

3.3.3.2 Divine Compulsion

PGM IV.2891–2942 exemplifies three ways in which the relationship between the γόης and the god to whom he appeals during the course of his operation can be defined by a vectored mode of ἀνάγκη leading from the former to the latter. The first point is that the word for "fulfill" used in the final section of the hymn, "τέλει" is the second-person imperative conjugation of τελέω. As mentioned earlier, this is not wholly uncommon either in κατάδεσμοι or ἀγωγαί, but it sets the tone for a framework within which the γόης is *commanding* Aphrodite to do something. Second, and more noticeable, is the spell's second section, where Aphrodite is directly threatened.

What is particularly interesting — and important in connecting ἀγωγή to θεαγωγία — is that this series of threats nicely mirrors the kinds of threats commonly made by the γόης against the victim of ἀγωγή spells. However, in this instance, the threats are being made against the *deity* effecting the spell's end goal. What this demonstrates is, thus, a direct continuity between the kinds of ἀγωγή spells wherein the γόης threatens a woman so that she comes to him and θεαγωγία spells where the deity is compelled to appear before the spell caster. Although in this instance, Aphrodite is not being caused to manifest — but is rather being coacted to cause *a woman* to manifest — the underlying ritual method, where the deity's actions are caused by the γόης, are identical.

3.3.3.3 The Importance of Ὀρκίζω

The third point, the use of the verb ὀρκίζω", is particularly important both because of the connotations carried by the word and owing to its prominence in the papyrological corpus. According to the *LMPG*,⁸⁷ ὀρκίζω" occurs some fifty-two times in the magical papyri.⁸⁸ Deriving from the word ὅρκος — which can either

---

⁸⁶Ibid., IV.2938–39.

⁸⁷*LMPG*, s.v. "ὀρκίζω."

⁸⁸Within the *PGM*, there are forty-four attestations: I.305, I.306, I.308, I.310, I.312, I.342, III.48, III.71, III.90, III.229, III.391, III.393, III.394,

3.3. ΑΝΑΓΚΗ AND SPELLS OF COMPULSION

refer to an oath, or the object by which that oath is sworn[89] — the LSJ defines ὁρκίζω in a general sense as to "make one swear" or to "administer an oath to a person," and in a "magical" sense as to "adjure."[90] The *LMPG* is more helpful in clarifying the term's usage within the *PGM*, giving two senses: (1) "conjurar, exigir la presencia para que se pongan al servicio del mago" (to conjure, to demand presence so as to be placed in the service of the magician), and (2) "conjurar, obligar mediante un conjuro" (to conjure, binding through a conjuration).[91]

Taken *in toto*, these definitions allow us to glean an important fact about this verbiage. Rather than implying a coercive relationship extending from the γόης toward the gods — as the previously examined instances of the use of second-person imperative verbs does — the term ὁρκίζω is quite explicit in defining a relationship in which the γόης binds the deity to his will by means of extracting an oath. Again, while this particular spell is not concerned with compelling a manifestation of Aphrodite, we can clearly see how such operations could emerge out of the same coercive atmosphere of the ἐπάναγκος variety of ἀγωγή spells.

IV.289, IV.345, IV.361, IV.396, IV.977, IV.978, IV.1551, IV.1557, IV.1708, IV.2312, IV.3018, IV.3033, IV.3037, IV.3045, IV.3039, IV.3058, IV.3062, IV.3065, IV.3075, IV.3078, IV.3081, IV.3205, VII.242, VII.246, VII.243, XII.84, XIII.278, XVI.17, XXXVI.153, XXXVI.250, XXXVI.258. Within the *SM*, there are seven attestations: 24.fr.a.1, 29.8, 46.5, 49.48, 50.48, 54.30, 57.1. Within the *Ostraka*, 1.6.

[89] *LSJ*, s.v. "ὅρκος."
[90] Ibid., s.v. "ὁρκίζω."
[91] *LMPG*, s.v. "ὁρκίζω."

Chapter 4
Psychagogy and Necromancy

4.1 From Ἔρως to Θάνατος

4.1.1 Compelling the Dead

In establishing a connection between the ἀγωγή spells discussed in the previous chapter and θεαγωγία, the cotemporal practice of ψυχαγωγία presents itself as a medial term in several important ways. The first point to be addressed is the way in which the erotic ἀγωγή spells bleed seamlessly into operations of necromantic ψυχαγωγία. This close connection is noted both by Johnston and Faraone. Johnston writes that in some situations ἀγωγή does not refer to the leading of a woman towards the spell caster, but rather to a category of "spells with which the γόητες can 'lead ghosts' against the living."[1]

This sentiment is echoed by Faraone, who notes that while ἀγωγή "usually refers to erotic spells designed 'to lead' women forcibly to men," in other circumstances within the *PGM* it "must refer to the 'leading' of ghosts or souls up from the underworld for a variety of purposes," making it "in short, to be the handbook equivalent of the word *psychagogia*."[2] As I have already detailed the close connections between the κατάδεσμοι

---
[1] Johnston, "Magic and the Dead in Classical Greece," 16.
[2] Faraone, "Necromancy Goes Underground," 258.

and ἀγωγαί on the one hand and between the κατάδεσμοι and ψυχαγωγία on the other, this section shall serve to demonstrate the fully entwined nature of all three practices by linking ἀγωγή to ψυχαγωγία.

4.1.2 Case Studies

4.1.2.1 *PGM* IV.1390–1495

This connection between the erotic ἀγωγή spells and the necromantic practices of ψυχαγωγία is most clearly illustrated in *PGM* IV.1390–1495. Titled, "Ἀγωγὴ ἐπὶ ἡρώων ἢ μονομάχων ἢ βιαίων" (Evocation by Violently Slain Heroes or Gladiators), the spell is — compared to the directly compulsive spells of the previous chapter — quite conventional in the relationship implied between the participants throughout its language. However, the spell differs in several key ways from the kinds of strictly erotic ἀγωγή spells we have previously examined. First, the rubric specifically identifies the location wherein the spell is to be performed — at the place where the categories of dead souls mentioned in the title "ἐσφάγησαν" (were slain).[3]

The spell's first major section consists of an invocation to Hecate which is to be said over the "ψωμούς" (morsels) left in sacrifice to the dead.[4] The invocation itself is not unusual, and bespeaks Hecate to "ἄξατε οὗ αὐτὴν βασανιζομένην, διὰ τάχους" (fetch her by means of torture, swiftly).[5] Granted, the use of ἄγω's second-person imperative, ἄξατε, does carry the kinds of coactive undertones discussed above; however, the overall tone of the hymn is supplicatory — speaking reverently to the goddess as "κυρία Ἑκάτη" (mistress Hecate).[6]

The γόης is then advised to wait three days to see if this first section of the spell achieves the desired result. If it does not, then he is advised to perform a second "ἐπανάγκῳ" (coercive

---

[3] *PGM*, IV.1394. For more on cemeteries as locations for necromantic operations, see Johnston, *Restless Dead*, 95–8.

[4] *PGM*, IV.1398–1434. For additional examples of food offerings being made to the Greek dead within a ritual context, see: Aristophanes, *Lysistrata*, 599–601; Plutarch, *Aristides*, 21.

[5] *PGM*, IV.1412–13.

[6] Ibid., IV.1433.

4.1. FROM ΕΡΩΣ ΤΟ ΘΑΝΑΤΟΣ

spell), which invokes a whole array of chthonic θεοί, "ὠμοφάγοι" (carnivores), "ἀμφίπολοι" (handmaidens), "πνεύματα" (spirits), "Ἁμαρτίαι" (sins), "Ὄνειροι" (dreams), "Ὅρκοι" (oaths), "Βασκανία" (charms), "ὀπάονες" (attendants), "νέκυες" (corpses), "δαίμονες" (daemons), and "ψυχαί" (souls).[7] This infernal host is directed to aid the γόης in effecting the accomplishment of his "ἀγωγῆς" (evocation), such that they will "ἄξητέ" (fetch) her to him.[8]

This point is strongly and forcefully re-emphasised, as the γόης petitions a number of underworld gods — including Chaos, Erebos, Hecate, Pluto, Kore, Hermes, the Moirai, Poine,[9] Aeacus,[10] and Anubis to "ἀναπέμψατέ μοι τῶν νεκύων τούτων εἴδωλα" (send forth to me the images of the ghosts of the dead) so that they might "πορευθέντες ἄξωσι μοι, τῷ δεῖνα" (go forth and fetch her, NN, to me).[11] Again, in establishing a broad theme of a generalised coactive undertone that pervades the ἀγωγή family of spells, it is worth noting that in this final command, it is the second-person imperative form of ἀναπέμπω (to send forth, or up) which is used to denote the γόης issuing a command to the chthonic gods.

4.1.2.2 PGM IV.2708–84

Lest we think this spell an aberration, it will serve to detail another instance of this formula in action. In PGM IV.2708–84, titled "Ἄλλη ἀγωγή" (Another Evocation), we see a much more simplified variation on the same theme. Here, after offering a mixture of cumin and goat-fat to Selene, the γόης invokes a syncretised amalgamation of Hecate, Kore, Artemis, Selene, Perse-

---

[7]Ibid., IV.1443–55.

[8]Ibid., IV.1456–57.

[9]Ποινή (retribution, vengeance) appears throughout classical literature as the daemonic embodiment of vengeance. For examples, see: Aeschylus, *Libation Bearers*, 937ff.; Flaccus, *Argonautica*, 7.147ff.

[10]Αἰακός (lamentation) is one of several minor deities associated with the judgment of the dead in Hades — typically seen serving as a gatekeeper. Characteristic examples can be seen in sources as disparate as Homer *Odyssea* 11.568ff. and Plato *Gorgias* 523a.

[11]Ibid., IV.1459–68.

Figure 4.1: The so-called "Burney Relief" (c. 1800–1750 BC), depicting a Babylonian underworld goddess, likely Ereshkigal. Photo by Aiwok, 2011.

phone, and Ereshkigal.[12] The spell is genuinely supplicative, rather than coercive — with the verbiage being in forms such as, "Ἑκάταν σε καλῶ" (Hecate, I call thee), indicating that the hymn is a request rather than a command.[13]

What is significant here is not that he calls on underworld deities, but rather that he calls for this goddess to bring with her "ἀποφθιμένοισιν ἀώροις" (untimely dead) and "ἡρώων ἔθανον ἀγύναιοί τε ἄπαιδες" (heroes who died wifeless and childless).[14] It is interesting to note that when the γόης addresses these dead souls, the verbs change from first-person present active indicative forms to second-person imperatives. In such an instance, the γόης commands the dead souls to "ἀφέλεσθε" (take away) sleep from his intended victim so that she will come to him to be freed from the torment of insomnia.[15]

4.1.3 Ritual Analysis

From these two spells, we can glean several facts which aid in our understanding of a continuum existing between erotic ἀγωγή spells and ψυχαγωγία. First, while neither of these spells operates as a strict representative of either category, each one participates in aspects of both. For example, while the simple ἀγωγή spell's relational complex is a triangle composed of the γόης, his intended victim, and the gods; and the simple ψυχαγωγία spell's relational complex is a triad of the γόης, the dead souls, and the gods; the intermediary varieties examined in this section have relational diagrams with four members: the γόης, his intended victim, the souls of the dead, and the gods.

Second, both spells illustrate ways in which coaction is present in the ἀγωγή and ψυχαγωγία rubrics. In this regard, we have seen that there is a great deal of variability within the ἀγωγή class itself and within the two hybrid spells analysed. In some instances, we have seen compulsion strictly enacted by the γόης onto a girl, using a deity as an intermediary transmitter. Yet in others, we have seen the coaction directed towards both the intended victim

---

[12]Ibid., IV.2714ff.
[13]Ibid., IV.2730.
[14]Ibid., IV.2731–33.
[15]Ibid., IV.2735–44.

and the gods. And still yet among the hybrid class, we see coercion directed towards both parties previously indicated as well as the souls of the dead.

Thus, while we do see a great deal of variability, it is variability strictly in terms of toward which target the coactive power of the γόης will be directed, rather than there being an real question of whether the operation will or will not incorporate a coercive element. Third — and most important at the present juncture — what these two hybrid spells exemplify is that the operative technology of ἀγωγή and ψυχαγωγία spells were not only *not* mutually exclusive, but at were at times identical. This last point ought to be borne in mind during the course of the next section where we begin to examine strict examples of ψυχαγωγία.

4.2 Corpse Animation and Soul Evocation

4.2.1 King Pitys the Necromancer

Having already discussed earlier both the hybrid ἀγωγή-ψυχαγωγία spells of the *PGM* as well as early Homeric instances of strict ψυχαγωγία, we may now in this section delve into strict ψυχαγωγία as it is presented in the later magical papyri. As with our prior investigations into the κατάδεσμοι and ἀγωγαί, the purpose of this foray is to gain an understanding of the connection that exists between this practice and θεαγωγία. To accomplish this, the bulk of this section will be composed of exegesis carried out on a series of spells from the Paris magical papyrus — all of which are attributed to the legendary King Pitys.

Now, Pitys (Πίτυς) — meaning "pine" — is a name belonging both to a nymph pursued by Pan,[16] as well as a figure mentioned in three spells in the *PGM*.[17] The papyri identify him as a Thessalian[18] King.[19] This attribution appears to be strictly legendary; as such a name is not recorded among the known Kings of Thessaly. However, Ogden does draw a connection between Pitys and Bitys (Βίτυς) — an equally legendary Egyptian

---

[16]Ovid, *Metamorphoses*, I.689ff.; Nonnus, *Dionysiaca*, II.108ff.
[17]*PGM*, IV.1928–2005, IV.2006–2125, IV.2140–44.
[18]Ibid., IV.2140.
[19]Ibid., IV.1928.

4.2. CORPSE ANIMATION AND SOUL EVOCATION

sage referenced both by Iamblichus and Zosimus of Panopolis (fourth century AD).[20] Iamblichus describes Bitys as an Egyptian "προφήτης" (prophet) and hermeneut who wrote treatises on Egyptian religion.[21] Zosimus describes Bitys' writings as being on par with those of Plato, Hermes Trismegistus, and the god Thoth.[22]

Speaking of these writings described by Iamblichus and Zosimus, Garth Fowden tells us that "clearly our two sources are talking about the same composition" — seeing in these references to Bitys' writings a late antique Egyptian analogue to the *Oracula Chaldaica*.[23] And, while the spells attributed to the Pitys of the *PGM* are more likely to be described as "magical"[24] — as opposed to the θεουργία of the *Oracula Chaldaica* — the largely Hermetic character of the magical papyri is at least somewhat consistent with the two descriptions of Bitys.

4.2.2 Two of Pitys' Spells

4.2.2.1 *PGM* IV.2140–44

The third spell of Pitys is the shortest — at only four lines — yet will serve well to set the tone for this discussion of ψυχαγωγία proper, as its end is wholly apart from the usual intended outcomes of both κατάδεσμοι and ἀγωγαί. Titled, "Πίτους Θεσσαλοῦ ἀνάκρισις σκήνους" (Pitys of Thessaly's Corpse Examinations),[25] the aim of this spell is quite simply to obtain answers from a corpse. The ritual mechanisms are quite simple, consisting only of two *nomina barbara* written onto a flax leaf with a specially prepared ink, which is then placed inside the mouth of the corpse to be animated.[26]

---

[20] Ogden, *Magic, Witchcraft, and Ghosts in the Greek and Roman Worlds*, 204; Ogden, *Greek and Roman Necromancy*, 211.

[21] Iamblichus, *On the Mysteries*, VIII.5.

[22] Zosimus, Περὶ ὀργάνων καὶ καμίνων γνήσια ὑπομνήματα περὶ τοῦ ω στοιχείου, 1–10, 75–6.

[23] Fowden, *The Egyptian Hermes*, 151.

[24] Indeed, in *PGM* IV.2081 the spell's practitioners are described as a "μάγων" (magicians).

[25] *PGM*, IV.2140. In the *GMPT*, W.C. Grese translates this title as, "Pitys the Thessalian's spell for questioning corpses."

[26] *PGM*, IV.2140–44.

What, however, is quite valuable to note in this spell is not the mechanics, but the aim: knowledge. Rather than attempting to bind a foe or woo a lover, the caster of this spell is seeking information about things currently unknown to him. This spell belongs to the category of νεκρομαντεία — dubbed "necromancy proper" by Ogden[27] — as it is quite literally a μαντεῖον (oracle) received from a νέκυς (corpse). While this is still rather far from the divine γνῶσις (knowledge) of the Hermetists and Gnostics,[28] it is yet a far cry from the bindings and fetchings of living people against their will. And, more importantly, the mantic orientation of the majority of these types of ψυχαγωγία establishes an immediate link between it and θεαγωγία — as prophecy is the goal of a great many of the latter spells as well.[29]

Even still — as separate as these aims are — there is a direct continuity between the underlying mechanism of the erotic ἀγωγή spells and this brand of ψυχαγωγία. For, both categories of spells achieve their respective goals by means of bringing a soul from elsewhere to the γόης. In the case of the ἀγωγή spell, the soul is clothed in the flesh of a woman and is being brought from her father's house; and, in the case of the ψυχαγωγία spell, the soul is that of a dead man being brought forth from the Underworld. However, in both types of operation, the generalised character is that of the γόης effecting motion in the soul of another towards him.

4.2.2.2 *PGM* IV.1928–2125

The first spell of Pitys, titled "Ἀγωγὴ Πίτους βασιλέως ἐπὶ παντὸς σκύφου" (Evocation of King Pitys through Any Skull-Cup), centers on obtaining prophecy from the reanimated skull of a corpse.[30] From the title alone, we see one significant feature already. Although this spell is, as we shall see momentarily, clearly

---

[27] Ogden, *Greek and Roman Necromancy*, xx.

[28] For γνῶσις in the Hermetic corpus, see: Fowden, *The Egyptian Hermes*, 104–15; Copenhaver, "Introduction," xxxvi–xl; van den Broek, "Gnosticisn and Hermetism in Antiquity," 1–20.

[29] This will be detailed in more length in chapter five, but a clear example of the acquisition of μαντεία (prophetic ability) as the goal of a θεαγωγός can be seen in: *PGM*, V.54–69.

[30] *PGM*, IV.1928–2005.

4.2. CORPSE ANIMATION AND SOUL EVOCATION 69

an example of strict ψυχαγωγία, it describes itself as an ἀγωγή spell—implying a direct line of continuity between ἀγωγή spells of erotic and necromantic varieties.

Unlike the previous spell, which strictly portrayed a coercive relationship existing between the γόης and the dead soul, *PGM* IV.1928–2005 appeals to Helios and his "ἁγίους σου ἀγγέλους" (holy angels).[31] The operator directly asks them to "δός μοι τὴν κατεξουσίαν τούτου τοῦ βιοθανάτου πνεύματος" (grant sovereignty to me over the spirit of one dead by violence) so that he may "κατέχω" (hold fast) the man's soul to keep as his "βοηθὸν" (assistant) and "ἔκδικον" (avenger).[32] While this line of instruction seems to be indicating that this spell's function is to acquire a general assistant,[33] the subsequent hymn to Helios clarifies the situation, instructing Helios to command the dead soul to "φρασάτω" (show) and "καταλέξῃ" (tell) him all manners of things with "ἀληθείῃ" (truth).[34] Additionally, the final section of the spell is sub-titled "ἀνάκρισις" (examination), which is exactly the same question-oriented noun that distinguishes *PGM* IV.2140–44 as a necromantic spell *par excellence*. Indeed, taken as a whole, these two spells are strongly linked in demonstrating the primary goal of ψυχαγωγία as effecting the transmission of knowledge from the dead by coactively evoking their souls.

One final point to be made regarding this spell reaches back to chapter two's discussion of the overlap between the Greek conceptions of dead souls and daemons. This linguistic blurring is remarkably apparent in this spell. As, during the course of the hymn to Helios, the γόης directly identifies the dead soul being evoked as a "δαίμονα" (daemon) from the "νεκύων τ' ἐπὶ χῶρον" (place of the dead).[35] As such, in this spell, we see a bridge forming between the strictly necromantic conception of

---

[31] Ibid., IV.1933–34.

[32] Ibid., IV.1948–49.

[33] Spells to summon "magical" assistants are rather common in the papyri. For examples, see: Ibid., I.1–42, XII.14–95, LVII.1–37. For more on this practice, see: Ciraolo, "Supernatural Assistants in the Greek Magical Papyri," 279–95; Pachoumi, "Divine Epiphanies of Paredroi in the Greek Magical Papyri," 155–65; Pachoumi, *The Concepts of the Divine in the Greek Magical Papyri*, 35–61.

[34] Ibid., IV.1971–72.

[35] Ibid., IV.1967–68.

evocating the souls of the dead that comprises ψυχαγωγία and the practice of θεαγωγία which evocates the divine beings — since, as we have seen, the lines between the daemons and gods could be as tenuously defined as those between the daemons and the dead.

4.3 An Exegesis of *PGM* IV.2006–2125

4.3.1 Pitys' Evocation

PGM IV.2006–2125 is the longest of the spells attributed to Pitys and is also the richest in detail. Simply titled, "Πίτους ἀγωγή" (Pitys' Evocation), this spell is a veritable *tour de force* — singularly bridging the gaps between erotic ἀγωγή, ψυχαγωγία, and θεαγωγία at once. The form taken by this spell is didactic, and presents itself as a set of instructions being given by Pitys to a King Ostanes.[36] Ostanes is a legendary figure, typically identified as a Persian king, who is variously credited with introducing alchemical and magical arts to the Greeks.[37]

The lesson begins with the construction of an elaborate circular design composed of dozens of *voces magicae* upon a dried ass' hide.[38] On the hide, the divine names are immediately followed by this printed evocation: "ἐξορκίζω σε, νεκύδαιμον, κατὰ τοῦ ἰσχυροῦ καὶ ἀπαραιτήτου θεοῦ καὶ κατὰ τῶν ἁγίων αὐτοῦ ὀνομάτων" (I conjure thee, dead daemon, by means of the strong and inexorable god and by means of his hallowed names).[39] After this object has been placed under the corpse to be animated, the dead soul is said to appear.[40]

Once this occurs, the operator is instructed to recite a further series of *voces magicae*,[41] followed by an explicit evocation similar to that previously printed on the ass' hide: "ἐξορκίζω

---

[36] Ibid., IV.2006.
[37] Van Bladel, *The Arabic Hermes*, 48–54. See also: Bidez and Cumont, *Les Mages hellénisés*, 1:165–212; Lindsay, *The Origins of Alchemy in Graeco-Roman Egypt*, 131–58.
[38] Ibid., IV.2014–31.
[39] Ibid., IV.2031–34.
[40] Ibid., IV.2034–53.
[41] Ibid., IV.2054–60.

σε, νεκύδαιμον, κατὰ τῆς Ἀνάγκης τῶν Ἀναγκῶν παραγενέσθαι πρὸς ἐμέ, τὸν δεῖνα" (I conjure thee, dead daemon, by means of the Necessity of Necessities, to be beside me, NN).[42] The γόης commands the dead soul, that if he does not agree to serve him, that he can "κολάσεις προσδόκα" (expect chastisements) to be forthcoming.[43]

4.3.2 A Coactive Operation

Thus, in this initial series of evocations, we see the coactive nature of ψυχαγωγία laid bare. The primary verb used, ἐξορκίζω is a slight variation on the already familiar ὁρκίζω — which revealed itself to be a paradigm of linguistic coercion in the ἀγωγή spells. Additionally, similar to the threats against Aphrodite in *PGM* IV.2891–2942, the γόης here directly threatens the νεκυδαίμων being evoked, explicitly making clear the coercive force implied by his conjuration's operative verb.

This particular mode of coercion is particularly interesting, as we actually see a description of the contractual force implied by the ἐξορκίζω/ὁρκίζω terminology. The rubric instructs the γόης to take a specially prepared "ἱερατικὸν κόλλημα γράφον" (hieratic papyrus roll) which has been inscribed with a figure not present in the manuscript, to write the spell previously spoken upon it, and to then offer it to the spirit.[44] This will, Pitys claims, immediately "ἄξει" (fetch) the νεκυδαίμων — binding him to the service of the spell caster.[45]

What appears to be going on in this odd description is that the papyrus roll is functioning as a sort of contract which, once accepted by the spirit, compels his appearance before the γόης. Remembering the primary definition of ὁρκίζω from the *LMPG*,[46] this appears to be a perfectly illustrated example of a contractual adjuration within the framework of a ψυχαγωγία spell — demon-

---

[42]Ibid., IV.2060–61.
[43]Ibid., IV.2064–65. For more on this spell, see: Pachoumi, *The Concepts of the Divine in the Greek Magical Papyri*, 42–3.
[44]Ibid., IV.2065–72.
[45]Ibid., IV.2072–74.
[46]"Conjurar, exigir la presencia para que se pongan al servicio del mago." This is also the exact same definition given in the *LMPG* for ἐξορκίζω.

strating clearly the direct coaction operating between the γόης and the νεκυδαίμων.

4.3.3 The Necro-Daemon

Of interest at this juncture in examining *PGM* IV.1928–2005 is the figure of the νεκυδαίμων (pl. νεκυδαίμονες). The *LSJ* defines this simply as the "ghost of a dead man," which seems accurate in this case, but is hardly as descriptive as it could be.[47] The *LMPG*, thankfully, provides a more elaborate definition: "demon de un muerto ser invocado en las prácticas para que se ponga al servicio del mago" (demon of the dead, to be invoked in practices so as to be placed in the magician's service).[48] The term appears some twenty-four times among the magical papyri,[49] being one of the most common means of denoting the evoked object of a ψυχαγωγία operation.

What is most interesting about the term is that it serves as a primary example of the variability of the daemonic concept within the ἀγωγή family of spells. As we have seen, in Pitys' spell above, the term clearly refers to the soul belonging to the corpse being animated. However, the three instances in *PGM* IV.296–466 all refer to one of the chthonic gods previously invoked to enact the erotic binding of the φιλτροκατάδεσμος spell. And yet, in other spells, such as *PGM* VII.993–1009, the context is rather ambiguous — leaving the question of whether the entity being evocated is a god, daemon (proper), or dead soul.

The significance of this linguistic ambiguity is important in that it further establishes the connected nature of ψυχαγωγία and θεαγωγία. For, if there exists a body of operative techniques designed to evocate νεκυδαίμονες *qua* dead souls, and the category of νεκυδαίμονες can be shown to refer to both dead souls and gods within the same papyrological corpus, then it can be reasonably implied that techniques in that same corpus that specifically de-

---

[47] *LSJ*, s.v. "νεκυδαίμων."

[48] *LMPG*, s.v. "νεκυδαίμων."

[49] Within the *PGM*, there are thirteen attestations: *PGM*, IV.361, IV.368, IV.397, IV.2031, IV.2061, V.334, VII.1006, XII.491, XVI.1, XIXa.15, LI.1, LI.5, LI.21. Within the *SM*, there are eleven attestations: *SM*, 39.1, 47.14, 47.18, 48.14, 48J.6, 48J.20, 48J.31, 49.28, 49.33, 50.12, 57.1.

4.3. AN EXEGESIS OF PGM IV.2006–2125

scribe methods of evocating gods exist on a continuum with their psychagogic counterparts.

4.3.4 Teleology

The final aspect of Pitys' second spell to be analysed here allows us to connect, within the context of explicitly necromantic spells, all three categories: ἀγωγή, ψυχαγωγία, and the κατάδεσμοι. The uses given for this spell of corpse reanimation are five-fold. The evocated νεκυδαίμων is said to perform the following functions for the γόης: "ἄγει δὲ καὶ κατακλίνει καὶ ὀνειροπομπεῖ καὶ κατέχει καὶ ὀνειραιτητεῖ" (he fetches, strikes with illness, sends dreams, binds, and gives revelations through dreams).[50] The second and fourth activities clearly connect to goals more closely associated with the κατάδεσμοι than anything else.

The verb κατακλίνω is defined in the *LSJ* within this specific context as to "cause one to take to his bed," which is a metaphor for to "strike with disease."[51] This is a wholly retributive kind of antagonistic spell that is not at all uncommon in the corpus of binding curses. The specific use of the verb κατέχω (to bind, or hold fast) in the fourth position cements this link — as it is the word for binding most commonly found in the κατάδεσμοι. The first term, ἄγω, is of course quite familiar at this point, and in this context most definitely refers to erotic evocation.

We know this not because of the isolated use of the verb in this sentence, but rather because of the following "λόγος" — meaning "spell" in this context — section wherein the "καταχθονίῳ δαίμονι" (chthonic daemon) is commanded to go to a particular girl's home and "ἄξον αὐτὴν πρὸς ἐμὲ τὸν δεῖνα" (bring her to me, NN).[52] This line of command is all but stereotypical of the erotic ἀγωγή spells detailed previously. And, although we have seen several prior instances of psychagogic means being used to effect either binding or erotic compulsion, it is quite telling — insofar as regarding the ways in which these practices were not segregated into discrete categories — that we see a both/and situation in this spell.

---

[50] *PGM*, IV.2076–78.
[51] *LSJ*, s.v. "κατακλίνω."
[52] *PGM*, IV.2088–91.

4.3.5 Necromantic Dream Divination

The third and fifth commands of this spell are, however, more specifically necromantic in their ends, and are also more generally characteristic of the ways in which necromancy was believed to function in antiquity. The first of the pair refers to the practice of ὀνειροπομπεία, which the *LMPG* defines as "envío de sueños" (sending dreams).[53] The second, ὀνειραιτησία, is a related term defined as "obtención de revelaciones en sueños" (obtaining revelations in dreams).[54] The first practice, ὀνειροπομπεία, is particularly associated with erotic ἀγωγή spells in which the γόης sends a dream to his intended victim designed to draw them to him.[55]

The clearest instance of this technique in action is the short, untitled spell *PGM* VII.407–10. Therein, the operator is instructed that if he wishes to "ἐμφανῆναι διὰ νυκτὸς ἐν ὀνείροις" (be seen through dreams at night) so that the woman he seeks to attract will "ἰδέτω με... ἐν τοῖς ὕπνοις" (see me in her slumbers), then he should frequently repeat two *voces magicae*. The second oneiric term, ὀνειραιτησία, is more closely linked to rituals which straddle the line between θεαγωγία and θεουργία. In *PGM* V.370–446, another untitled spell, the practitioner is directed to craft a "πλάσμα ἑρμοῦ" (figure of Hermes) out of a variety of materials within which is then placed a spell written on hieratic papyrus (or on the windpipe of a goose).[56] This statue is to be placed in a specially crafted shrine by which the operator sleeps.[57] He then, while going to sleep, recites a spell petitioning Hermes to "φάνηθι" (appear)[58] to him in his dreams so as to partake in

---

[53] *LMPG*, s.v. "ὀνειροπομπεία." For discussion of this practice, see: Eitrem, "Dreams and Divination in Magical Ritual," 179–82; Dodson, *Reading Dreams*, 24.

[54] *LMPG*, s.v. "ὀνειραιτησία." For discussion of this practice, see: Eitrem, "Dreams and Divination," 176–79; Renberg, *Where Dreams May Come*, 2:717–44.

[55] Winkler, "The Constraints of Eros," 229; Eitrem, "Dreams and Divination," 180–81.

[56] *PGM*, V.370–90.

[57] *PGM*, V.390–97.

[58] Ibid., V.418. As with so many spells from the *PGM*, this operative verb appears in the second-person imperative form.

4.3. AN EXEGESIS OF PGM IV.2006–2125

the god's skills in "μαντοσύναις" (divination).[59]

While the τελεστική component of this has led at least one scholar to make tentative connections to θεουργία,[60] the spell's final two sections seem to imply a deeper connection to the θεαγωγία rituals. The second to last section is titled, "Ἐπάναγκος," and is otherwise composed almost wholly of *nomina barbara*.[61] The final section, titled "Ἄλλη" (Another) — which refers to it being another coactive ἐπάναγκος spell — is similarly composed, summating with a command to Hermes: "εἴσελθε καὶ χρημάτισον" (come in [to my dreams] and give oracles).[62]

4.3.6 Ψυχαγωγία, Θεαγωγία, and Ἀγωγή

Taken within the context of *PGM* IV.2006–2125, the presence of oneiric ritual mechanics which pertain to both ἀγωγή and θεαγωγία operations is quite telling in terms of understanding the relationship between these two practices and ψυχαγωγία. Although Pitys' spell is principally necromantic, we see in it strong echoes of the ἀγωγή spells we have analysed previously and the θεαγωγία rites with which the subsequent chapter deals.

As such, this spell in particular — as well as Pitys' other spells — demonstrates clearly the position that many of the ψυχαγωγία spells fill as being a sort of nexus between the seemingly disparate domains of erotic and divine spell casting. Given the connections previously detailed between the κατάδεσμοι and ψυχαγωγία on the one hand, between ἀγωγή and ψυχαγωγία on another, between ἀγωγή and θεαγωγία on yet another, and between ψυχαγωγία and θεαγωγία on still another, it should come as no real surprise that there exist examples such as this which harmonize all of the above elements into an organic unity.

What this demonstrates is that all four practices were viewed

---

[59] Ibid., V.419.

[60] Krulak, "The Animated Statue and the Ascension of the Soul," 46. For more general information on dreams in θεουργία, see: Athanassiadi, "Dreams, Theurgy and Freelance Divination," 115–30; Addey, "Oracles, Dreams and Astrology in Iamblichus' *De mysteriis*," 35–58.

[61] *PGM*, V.435–9.

[62] Ibid., V.440–6. It is, again, worth noting here that εἴσελθε is the second-person imperative of εἰσέρχομαι (to go in), underscoring the implicit coercion of this spell's syntax.

by those who practiced them — and likely by external observers among the medical and philosophical communities — as a family of related operations which could flow seamlessly into one another when a particular spell demanded it. And it is, I believe, only with this understanding of the interrelated nature of all members of the greater ἀγωγή family of spells that any one member can be fully understood.

Chapter 5

Evocating the Gods

5.1 Θεαγωγία and the *Pḥ-nṯr* Spells of the *PDM*

5.1.1 Linguistic Roots of *Pḥ-nṯr*

Among all of these related terminologies, it is *pḥ-nṯr* which bears the closest inspection in clarifying both the origins of and mechanisms by which θεαγωγία is seen to operate within *PGM* IV.930–1114. The term itself is a compound of two individual words. The first, *pḥ*, is a verb meaning "to reach, arrive (at)."[1] The second, *nṯr*, is a noun, referring to a "god."[2] Taken together, this compound implies something having to do with a god's arrival.

Janet H. Johnson translates this as "petitioning (lit. 'reaching') god" — noting it as a "term for direct oracular communication w. deity."[3] Johnson also importantly notes that in in F.L. Griffith and Herbert Thompson's *Demotic Magical Papyrus of London and Leiden*, the term *pḥ-nṯr* is mistranscribed as *wḥe-nṯr*, where *wḥe* signifies "letter."[4] This being the case, all references to *pḥ-nṯr* which refer to Griffith and Thompson's edition of the Demotic papyri will read in his edition as *wḥe-nṯr*, although we now know that *pḥ-nṯr* is the correct reading. Jacco Dielman,

---
[1] *CDD*, s.v. "pḥ."
[2] Ibid., s.v. "nṯr."
[3] Ibid., s.v. "pḥ(e) nṯr."
[4] Johnson, "Louvre E 3229," 90.

Ian Moyer, as well as the English translations of the *PDM* in the *GMPT* all translate *pḥ-nṯr* as a spell concerned with a "god's arrival."[5] Robert Ritner, however, argues that this definition of "god's arrival" is flawed,[6] and that "the literal meaning of *pḥ-nṯr*" is "to reach god," expanding this to denote the sense of "a direct confrontation and communication with the deity" and "an oracular divine audience."[7]

What is most important for our understanding of θεαγωγία is the nature of the syncretic connection that resulted in the identification of the Greek terms with the Demotic *pḥ-nṯr*. Although it is clear that the Greek notion of "magic" — qua μαγεία, γοητεία and their Roman adaptions *magia* and *goetia* — did not exist in Egypt until the Coptic period (first century AD),[8] *pḥ-nṯr* appears to be a native Egyptian practice which existed prior to the Graeco-Roman incursions.[9]

5.1.2 Egyptian Magical Theory

The ultimately Egyptian origin of the *pḥ-nṯr* spells is of great importance in tracing the origin of the coercive elements that play so heavily in θεαγωγία spells. While Fowden's assertions that "it is to ancient Egypt that we should look for the origin of the idea that the magician could constrain the gods to do his will by abuse and threats,"[10] or that "the Greek magical formulae... can only be explained in terms of Egyptian antecedents,"[11] may be a bit ambitious, there are certainly important points worth noting.

First among these is Ritner's analysis of the term *pḥr*, which is generally a verb used to connote "to encircle, go around."[12] Rit-

---

[5]Dielman, "Scribal Practices in the Production of Magic Handbooks in Egypt," 108; Moyer, "Thessalos of Tralles and Cultural Exchange," 48; instances in the *PDM* are at every instance of the term occurring identified in the below ff. 374.

[6]Ritner, "Egyptian Magical Practice Under the Roman Empire," 3346.

[7]Ritner, *The Mechanics of Ancient Egyptian Magical Practice*, 214.

[8]Ritner, "Egyptian Magical Practice Under the Roman Empire," 3355, 3358; Ritner, *The Mechanics of Ancient Egyptian Magical Practice*, 220.

[9]Ritner, "Egyptian Magical Practice Under the Roman Empire," 3346; Moyer, "Thessalos of Tralles and Cultural Exchange," 49.

[10]Fowden, *The Egyptian Hermes*, 80–81.

[11]Ibid., 66.

[12]*CDD*, s.v. "pḥr."

5.1. ΘΕΑΓΩΓΙΑ AND THE PḤ-NṮR SPELLS OF THE PDM

ner interprets this act of encircling as underlying "an elaborate complex of magical conceptions which culminate in the adoption of the term as an expression for 'enchanting.'"[13] It is in this Egyptian term that we see the closest analogue to the Greek conception of the ἀνάγκη, in that it can at once refer to the divine governing of the cosmos and to spells which bind third parties — with the common theme being coercion.[14] This *pḫr* practice can be placed within the broader context of the ways in which names were treated in Egyptian theology to understand better the coercive mechanism by which the *pḥ-nṯr* spells operate. Not dissimilar to some later Platonic conceptions of the relationship between names and the object signified by them,[15] was the Egyptian notion that "an object's or being's whole nature was implicit in its name."[16]

It is, Ritner asserts, within this context that "the effectiveness of 'magical' words and names must be understood" — as in many instances, knowledge of the "true" name of a being was seen as imparting some degree of control over it.[17] A great many of the *voces magicae* with which the spells in the magical papyri compel women, ghosts, daemons, angels, and gods to do their bidding are of Egyptian origin. Betz identifies numerous examples of these throughout his footnotes to the *GMPT*. A good example of this can be seen in *PGM* I.42–195, where Betz identifies "Ἀμοῦν τε" as "Egyptian for Horus... Amon"; "πιχαρουρ" as "Egyptian for *pikrour*, 'the frog'"; and "Ἀμοῦν ω ῃϊ" as "Egyptian meaning 'Amon the Great.'"[18] This Egyptian aspect of the spells of the *PGM* and *PDM* allows us better understand how a native Egyptian practice such as *pḥ-nṯr* was syncretized with the native Greek traditions of coercive ἀγωγή spells to form the syncretic Graeco-Egyptian θεαγωγία which is so strongly represented in the papyri.

---

[13] Ritner, *The Mechanics of Ancient Egyptian Magical Practice*, 67.

[14] For the evolution of this term within Egyptian "magic," see Ritner, *The Mechanics of Ancient Egyptian Magical Practice*, 57–67.

[15] For discussion on this matter, see: van den Berg, *Proclus' Commentary on the Cratylus in Context*.

[16] Fowden, *The Egyptian Hermes*, 63–64.

[17] Ritner, *The Mechanics of Ancient Egyptian Magical Practice*, 247–49.

[18] Betz, *The Greek Magical Paypri in Translation*, 6, frr. 28, 29, 30. For more on this topic, see also: Love, *Code-Switching with the Gods*, 114–16.

5.1.3 Spells in the Demotic Corpus

This Demotic term appears as or in the titles of four spells within the *PDM*.[19] The four spells indicated here are all very strongly similar to *PGM* IV.930–1114, in that they are all spells in which the operator is instructed to coercively evoke a particular god, so as to obtain an oracle, either in the form of a lychnomantic or hydromantic oracle. The spell at *PDM Suppl.* 149–62 will serve as an exemplar. Titled "A God's Arrival" (w^c $pḥ$-$n\underline{t}r$),[20] this spell is an evocation of the god Thoth. The operator begins by calling to Thoth by means of a series of epithets, and then by a string of non-Demotic *nomina barbara* of unknown origin.[21] Following this, the operator commands the god: "Awaken to me, O lord of truth! Tell me an answer in truth to the 'god's arrival.'"[22] The operator is then given special instructions to prepare a lamp in whose flame the god will manifest once the evocatory formula has been said eight times.[23]

The similarities here to *PGM* 930–1114 are stark and point to a relationship that is at least analogical if not homological. In both cases, the essence of the spells involve an operator petitioning and then commanding a god, by means of *nomina barbara*, to appear before him within a flame and to then grant a prophecy. The fact that all of the $pḥ$-$n\underline{t}r$ spells within the *PDM* bear such strong morphological similarity to the θεαγωγία, αὔτοπτος, and σύστασις spells of the *PGM* leads us to the conclusion that the connection between them is not merely analogical, but is homological in nature — particularly given the fact that the $pḥ$-$n\underline{t}r$ form predates the Greek.

---

[19] Moyer, "Thessalos of Tralles and Cultural Exchange," 48: *PDM*, xiv.117–49; xiv.232–38; *PDM Suppl.*149–62, 162–68. Additionally, there are two spells which contain internal sections dealing with $pḥ$-$n\underline{t}r$ (*PDM*, xiv.150–231; xiv.805–40).

[20] "Louvre E 3229," 6.6 (trans. Johnson).

[21] Ibid., 6.7–10 (trans. Johnson).

[22] Ibid., 6.11 (trans. Johnson).

[23] Ibid., 6.13–16 (trans. Johnson).

5.1. ΘΕΑΓΩΓΙΑ AND THE PḤ-NṮR SPELLS OF THE PDM

5.1.4 Bilingual Graeco-Egyptian Spells

This connection between the Demotic and Greek terms is deepened when we look to the bilingual spells of the magical papyri. *PDM* xiv.93–114 [*PGM* XIVa.1–11] proves itself to be a singularly remarkable spell in that it demonstrates at once the aforementioned ambiguity between the δαίμων and θεός within the context of an ἀγωγή spell, as well as the interrelation between the Demotic *pḥ-nṯr* and Greek formulas of evocation.[24] The Demotic portion of the spell describes its function as *pḥ-nṯr*, and while this would seem to indicate that the object of this spell's evocation would be a god — and, indeed, the Greek portion describes the subject as being in the midst of the "θεὸν μέγαν" (vast gods)[25] — there are two anomalies.

First, the spell later identifies the subject to be evocated as one of the "ἀρχάγγελον" (archangels) of the aforementioned gods.[26] However, the end of the spell describes the operation as a "ψυχαγωγαίου" operation. Thus, we have two very interesting phenomena occurring here. On the one hand, although this connection is being made in a somewhat roundabout way via the intermediary Demotic term *pḥ-nṯr*, we see a near direct identification between ψυχαγωγία and θεαγωγία here. Additionally, the archangel being called in the spell is conjured by means of a daemon's intermediacy: "ἐξορκίζω σε κατὰ τοῦ... δαίμονος ὑψίστου" (I conjure you by the... loftiest daemon).[27] Thus, while the spell at once demonstrates an interrelation between ψυχαγωγία, θεαγωγία, and *pḥ-nṯr*, it also bespeaks a similar relationship between the categories of daemons, archangels, and gods.

Moreover, this conjuration of the archangel by means of the daemon's intermediacy represents an interesting transversal of the ordinary hierarchy that exists between these categories of entities. In what is perhaps the most concise statement on the late antique theory behind evocation, Iamblichus writes: "Ἀεὶ γὰρ ἐν τῇ θεουργικῇ τάξει διὰ τῶν ὑπερεχόντων τὰ δεύτερα καλεῖται" (For

---

[24] Within the *PGM* and *PDM* the two components of this spell are presented separately. They are shown as a unified whole within the *GMPT*.

[25] *PGM*, XIVa.4.

[26] Ibid., XIVa.5.

[27] Ibid., XIVa.7–9.

in the theurgic hierarchy, it is always the case that secondary beings are called through the intermediacy of their superiors).[28] This is to say that the operator should always *evoke* a given entity through the intermediacy of an *invocation* of a being set in governance over the evoked target. For example, to evoke a Jovian daemon, the operator should first invoke the god Jupiter. However, in this spell, we see the operator being instructed to evoke an archangel. As archangels are classified as superiors to daemons in nearly all antique hierarchies which include both classes,[29] this spell seems to represent an interesting transversal either of the usual hierarchical order of these classes, or of the formula of evocation itself.

5.2 An Exegesis of *PGM* IV.930–1114

5.2.1 The Spell's Title

As mentioned in preceding section, θεαγωγία is an incredibly rare term. Within the *PGM*, there are exactly two occurrences — both of which are found within the spell, *PGM* IV.930–1114. What follows is an exegesis of this spell geared specifically towards pulling out the contextualized meaning of θεαγωγία within the papyri. Titled "Αὔτοπτος," the spell is quite long and complex, being divided into twelve sections, and is at its core an evocation of the god Horus (in his form as Harpocrates) to visible appearance. This word, αὔτοπτος, is defined in the *LSJ* as "self-revealed"[30] — which does not tell us much on its face — and is a technical term found throughout the papyri.

This technical sense is clarified in the *LMPG*, in which it is translated generally as that "que proporciona una visión directa" (which provides a direct vision). In the specific sense of this spell this "vision" is clarified as referring "esp. de la divinidad" (especially of divinity), and is characterized as "de una fórmula" (a formula).[31] This special sense is maintained by the critical Ger-

---

[28] Iamblichus, *On the Mysteries*, IX.9.284
[29] Plaisance, "Of Cosmocrators and Cosmic Gods," 66–67; Dillon, *The Middle Platonists*, 46–47, 172
[30] *LSJ*, s.v. "αὔτοπτος."
[31] *LMPG*, s.v. "αὔτοπτος."

5.2. AN EXEGESIS OF PGM IV.930–1114

man and English editions, which both translate the title in ways which denote it referring to a direct vision.[32] Just as "Ἀγωγή," is the standard title in the Greek magical papyri for spells relating to erotic compulsion, so is "Αὔτοπτος," the standard for those relating to obtaining direct visions of the gods — appearing in the titles of four spells.[33]

5.2.2 Section I

5.2.2.1 Defining Σύστασις

The first section is titled "Σύστασις," which is yet another technical term — albeit with a much more multifaceted constellation of meanings attached to it. The word itself has the general meaning of "bringing together," and can refer to such instances of togetherness as "standing together," "close combat," or "power of attorney."[34] However, within the contexts of the magical papyri, the notion of some mode of "communication between a man and god,"[35] with a general emphasis on the communication taking the shape of a meeting or encounter,[36] is more apt.

Outside of the *PGM* — where the term is used frequently[37] — σύστασις is one of the more commonly employed technical terms found within literature on θεουργία,[38] and is attested both

---

[32] Preisendanz, in the *PGM*, translates it as "Vision in wachen Zustand" (Vision in the Waking State). Grese and O'Neil in the GMPT translate it as "Charm that produces a direct vision."

[33] *PGM*, IV.930–1114 detailed above; V.54–69, titled "Αὔτοπτος λογος" (Direct Vision Spell); VII.319–34, titled "Αὔτοπτος"; VII.335–47, titled "Αὐτοπτική" (Relating to a Direct Vision); VII.727–39, titled "Ἀπόλλωνος αὔτοπτος" (A Direct Vision of Apollo). Additionally, *PGM* Va.1–3 is untitled, but tells the operator that he will "αὐτοπτήσεις" (obtain a direct vision), indicating that the title may have been "Αὔτοπτος" or something similar.

[34] *LSJ*, s.v. "σύστασις."

[35] Ibid.

[36] *LMPG*, s.v. "σύστασις," defines it as either "comunicación, encuentro con la divinidad" (communication, meeting with the deity) or a "fórmula para conseguir un encuentro con la divinidad" (formula for an encounter with the deity).

[37] *PGM*, III.197, III.494, IV.779, IV.930, VI.1, VI.39.

[38] Johnston, *Hekate Soteira*, 88. For more on σύστασις as possession, see: Addey, "Divine Possession and Divination in the Graeco-Roman World," 171–185.

Figure 5.1: A statue in cast bronze of Horus, as Harpocrates, seated on a lotus (664–322 BC), from the Walters Art Museum collection (54.419). Photo by the Walters Art Museum, 2012.

5.2. AN EXEGESIS OF PGM IV.930–1114

in the *Oracula Chaldaica*³⁹ as well as in Proclus⁴⁰ as a means by which the θεουργός is united with the invocated god. The picture that emerges from these texts is that σύστασις was conceived of as a practice by which the operator could either invoke a god, conjoining with it himself (as in the *Oracula Chaldaica* and Proclus), or evocate a god, effecting its manifestation external to himself (as in the *PGM*). This terminological ambiguity at once calls to mind the "lower" arts of evocation and the "higher" arts of invocation that is characteristic of *PGM* IV.930–1114.

5.2.2.2 An Αὐτοψία Hymn

This σύστασις section details where and when the spell is to be performed, what type of dress the operator should adopt, and contains a small hymn which is more supplicative than one might expect from a spell such as this.⁴¹ After several lines of interspersed poetic epithets and *voces magicae*, the hymn petitions the god to hear him through the "αὐθοψίας" spell he is casting, and to reveal himself unto the operator through the "αὐτόπτου" spell.⁴² There are two points of immediate interest here. First, we see that the author is emphasizing a terminological unity between σύστασις and αὔτοπτος by describing the actions within the σύστασις section as being an αὔτοπτος.

Given the connections that exist between these two terms and the Demotic *pḥ-nṯr*, this is a significant statement of identity that will bear remembering when we come to the relationship between *pḥ-nṯr* and θεαγωγία. Second, the compiler of *PGM* IV makes a very interesting choice in utilizing the term "αὐθοψίας" in this line. Only appearing twice in the papyri,⁴³ this term appears to be synonymous with αὔτοπτος, indicating a spell to obtain a direct vision of the deity.⁴⁴

---

³⁹Majercik, "Introduction," 25; *The Chaldean Oracles*, fr. 208: "For (Proclus) made use of the 'conjunctions' [συστάσεσι], prayers, and the divine, ineffable, magic wheels of the Chaldeans" (trans. Majercik).
⁴⁰Proclus, *Procli Diadochi in Platonis rem publicam commentarii*, II.11.18.
⁴¹*PGM*, IV.930–54.
⁴²Ibid., IV.949–53.
⁴³Ibid., IV.950; XIII.734.
⁴⁴*LMPG*, s.v. "αὐτοψία."

5.2.2.3 Lychnomancy

The final line of the hymn is also of interest in that it indicates the mechanism by which the manifestation of the god being evocated (who has yet to be named directly) will be received. The spell specifically mentions that the goal of this αὔτοπτος is "λυχνομαντίας," which the *LMPG* defines as a type of "adivinación por medio de una lámpara" (divination by means of a lamp) — or lychnomancy.[45] Lychnomantic divination refers to the practice whereby the magician gazes into the fire to utilize it as a medium through which the object of his evocation can manifest.

Such techniques are not uncommon within the magical papyri,[46] but are thought to derive from the yet earlier practice of πυρομαντεία (divination by fire, pyromancy) which is attested from very early periods of Greek history onward. Johnston suggests that the connection between lychnomancy and pyromancy is such that the former is a scaled down version of the latter, and that such "scaled down temple-based procedures for use in domestic settings" were characteristic techniques of the γόητες.[47]

5.2.3 Section II

This first section bleeds almost seamlessly into the second — which is titled "Φωταγωγία" (Evocation of Light) — suggesting that λυχνομαντεία and φωταγωγία were thought by the compiler(s) of *PGM* IV to be synonymous.[48] The presence of φωταγωγία in a θεαγωγία spell is extremely interesting at this juncture, namely owing to the tremendous importance that the former plays in Iamblichus' θεουργία. During this portion of the spell, the operator is instructed to close his eyes and repeat an invocation to the god who is the "ἀόρατον φωτὸς γεννήτορα" (unseen begetter of light)[49] so that he will "εἴσελθε ἐν τῷ πυρὶ τούτῳ καὶ ἐνπνευμάτωσον αὐτὸν θείου πνεύματος καὶ δεῖξόν μοί σου τὴν

---

[45] Ibid., s.v. "λυχνομαντεῖον."
[46] For examples, see: *PGM*, VII.540–78; *PDM*, xiv.150–231, xiv.459–75, xiv.475–88, xiv.489–515, xiv.516–27.
[47] Johnston, *Ancient Greek Divination*, 158–9.
[48] Ibid., 158; Johnston, "*Homo fictor deorum est*," 412.
[49] *PGM*, IV.959–60.

5.2. AN EXEGESIS OF PGM IV.930–1114

ἀλκήν" (come in to this fire, inspire it with divine spirit, and show forth unto me thy strength).[50]

As we see that the solar deity is here seen to be transmitting πνεῦμα (spirit, or breath) into the fire to make himself manifest to the practitioner, there is a clear analogue to a section of *PGM* IV.475–829 — the so-called "Mithras Liturgy." Therein, the reader is instructed to "ἀνασπῶν" (draw in) the "ἀκτίνων πνεῦμα" (rays of spirit, or breath) during the course of an anagogic ascent towards the solar god.[51] Regarding this passage, Betz proposes that — given the double meaning of πνεῦμα as either "spirit" or "breath" — that this is referring to a technique where "the spirit is to be drawn in with the breath" as "transmitted by the rays of the sun."[52] The narrow technical similarities between the sections of these two spells serves to demonstrate the fact that, at least within the context of *PGM* IV, ἀναγωγή and θεαγωγία were not seen as mutually exclusive operations.

5.2.4 Section III

The third section of *PGM* IV.930–1114 is sub-titled "Κάτοχος τοῦ φωτός" (That Which Restrains the Light),[53] and serves as a bridge between the φωταγωγία and θεαγωγία sections. It notes that the importance of binding the evocated light to oneself lie in the fact that "ἐνίοτε γάρ σου καλοῦντος τὸν θεαγωγὸν λόγον σκοτία γίνεται" (at times when you intone the god-evocating spell, darkness is generated).[54] It is here that the evocator speaks his first word of command, addressing the light: "ὁρκίζω σέ, ἱερὸν φῶς, ἱερὰ αὐγή... παράμεινόν μοι" (I adjure you, holy light, holy light of the sun...stay beside me).[55] This warning about darkness-bringing gods is quite curious, particularly as the god with which this spell deals has already been identified as being he from whom the light itself emanates.

---

[50] Ibid., IV.965–57.
[51] Ibid., IV.538.
[52] Betz, *The "Mithras Liturgy,"* 130–31. See also: Johnston, "*Fiat lux, fiat ritus,*" 14.
[53] *PGM*, IV.973–85.
[54] Ibid., IV.977.
[55] Ibid., IV.978–80.

There are several possible solutions to this — all of which draw on Iamblichus. First, in *De mysteriis*, during his discussion of the epiphanies of the superior classes,[56] Iamblichus describes the gods as being so vast that they "οὐρανὸν ὅλον ἐνίοτε ἀποκρύπτειν καὶ τὸν ἥλιον καὶ τὴν σελήνην" (at time hide the whole of heaven and the sun and moon).[57] In their notes, the editors of the most recent edition of *De mysteriis* connect this passage to our present subject of exegesis, *PGM* IV.930–1114, noting that the spatial dimensions with which the evocated light is described[58] mirror the tremendous proportions of the gods in *De mysteriis*.[59] The second way we might explain this is to interpret the darkness as indicating the presence of daemons, who must be driven away by the divine light. This too is a notion found in *De mysteriis*, when Iamblichus tells us that when the gods "ἐπιλαμπόντων" (shine), that the "κακὸν καὶ δαιμόνιον" (evil and daemonic) beings give way "ὥσπερ φωτὶ σκότος" (even as the darkness [gives way] to light).[60]

The third possibility comes directly from one of Iamblichus' discussions of φωταγωγία in *De mysteriis*, where we are told that at times such evocations of the divine light are effected by means of the principle of contrary receptivity, in which the "φωταγωγοῦντες" (evocators of light) often "σκότος συνεργὸν λαμβάνουσιν" (utilize darkness as a tool).[61] It is my opinion that this final option, wherein the operator makes use of darkness as a means to more greatly emphasize and intensify the φωταγωγία — just as a black canvas intensifies the effect of white paint — makes the most sense in the context of *PGM* IV.930–1114. However, the situation is far from clear.

---

[56] For a full discussion of this section of *De mysteriis*, see: Clarke, *Iamblichus' De mysteriis*, 100–18; Plaisance, "Of Cosmocrators and Cosmic Gods," 64–85.
[57] Iamblichus, *On the Mysteries*, II.4.75.
[58] *PGM*, IV.970.
[59] Iamblichus, *On the Mysteries*, ff. 125.
[60] Ibid., III.31.176.
[61] Ibid., III.14.133.

5.2.5 Section IV

It is in the next, fourth, section of the spell that the proper θεαγωγία portion of the rite begins. Titled, "Θεαγωγὸς λόγος" (God-Evocating Spell),[62] this is the first instance where the god being evocated is named directly. Here, the operator speaks: "ἐπικαλοῦμαί σε, τὸν μέγιστον θεόν, δυνάστην Ὧρον Ἁρποκράτην" (I summon you, mighty god, lord Horus Harpocrates).[63] The operative verb used here, ἐπικαλέω, which can — within the context of defining a relationship between a man and god — be variously translated as to "summon," "invoke," or "invite."[64]

While this verb is not necessarily compulsive in nature, the further conjurations of the god within the θεαγωγὸς λόγος certainly indicate a coercive attitude. For, five times, the operator repeats the evocation, "εἴσελθε, φάνηθί μοι, κύριε" (come forth and appear to me, lord), within this section of the spell.[65] Both verbs, εἰσέρχομαι (to go, or come in) and φαίνω (to cause to appear), appear in second-person imperative forms, giving the evocation a clear sense of coercion through the repetition of this command. However, as in many indications of evocative coercion as we have seen thus far, it is in the fifth section that the situation is hypertrophied.

5.2.6 Section V

Titled, "Ἐπάναγκος" (Coercive Formula),[66] this short section functions to compel Horus to appear "ἐάν πως βραδύνῃ" (if he in any way delays).[67] Of this type of spell, Graf notes:

> There also exists a separate class of spells and rituals labeled ἐπάναγκοι (coercive procedures). [...] In most instances, the coercive spell or ritual is not the rule but a sort of last straw for the magician — when the invoked divinity does not arrive quickly enough

---

[62] *PGM*, IV.986–87.
[63] Ibid., IV.987–88.
[64] *LSJ*, s.v. "ἐπικαλέω."
[65] *PGM*, IV.1002; IV.1007; IV.1015; IV.1019; IV.1023–4.
[66] Ibid., IV.1036.
[67] *PGM*, IV.1036–37.

[as in *PGM* IV.1035], when the praxis after several repetitions brings no result [as in *PGM* II.45], when the divinity appears threatening and dangerous [as in *PGM* IV.3112].[68]

This direct compulsion of the god to appear before the operator is achieved by means of the intercession of a yet greater god, in whose name Horus is commanded. The spell caster tells Horus that "ἐπιτάσσει σοι ὁ μέγας ζῶν θεός" (you are commanded by the great living god), naming "Ἰάω αωϊ ωϊα αϊω ϊωα ωαϊ" (IAŌ AŌI ŌIA AIŌ IŌA ŌAI) as this god. He then says to Horus again to "εἴσελθε, φάνηθί μοι" (come forth and appear to me), adding this time that the god is to appear "ὅτι σε ἐξορκίζω κατὰ τοῦ κυρίου" (because I adjure you by the lord) and repeating a variation of the *nomina barbara*.[69] If there had been any lingering doubts over whether or not *PGM* IV.930–1114 were coercive in nature, such concerns ought now be assuaged.

5.2.7 Sections VI–VIII

The spell's sixth section, "Χαιρετισμός" (Salutation), is of little interest here as it is simply a ritualized greeting.[70] The seventh section, however, is more interesting. It is the theagogic cognate to the photagogic retention spell in part three. Titled, "Κάτοχος τοῦ θεοῦ" (That Which Restrains a God), this seemingly bizarre section advises the operator to step on the god's big toe with his heel so that he will be unable to leave unless the operator lifts his foot.[71] It is incredibly plain that the god is being approached in a way wholly coercive, as he is quite literally being held in place. Granted, this odd line could be taken metaphorically — but even so, the general sense of coercion would have to remain.

In any event, the reader is advised that the god will remain in his presence until he lifts his foot and speaks the dismissal portion of the spell. This is found in the eighth section, appropriately titled, "Ἀπόλυσις" (Loosing, or Release)[72] — which in

---

[68]Graf, "Prayer in Magic and Religious Ritual," 194.
[69]Ibid., IV.1038–46.
[70]Ibid., IV.1046–52.
[71]Ibid., IV.1051–56.
[72]Ibid., IV.1057.

this context has the specific sense of being a "spell for releasing a divine being."⁷³ This section is relatively simple consisting of the operator systematically divesting himself of his tools, lifting his heel from Horus' toe, closing his eyes, and thrice thanking the god and commanding him to (in the second-person imperative, as usual): "χώρει" (begone).⁷⁴

5.2.8 Sections IX–XII

Following this, the ninth section — titled "Τῆς αὐγῆς ἀπόλυσις" (Loosing the Light) — speaks similarly to the previously evocated light: "χώρει, ἱερὰ αὐγή" (begone, holy light).⁷⁵ The tenth and eleventh sections, titled "Φυλακτήριον τῆς πράξεως" (Phylactary for the Ritual)⁷⁶ and "Ποίησις" (Method of Procedure)⁷⁷ respectively, work together to describe the production and consecration of an amulet which is to be worn during the rite for protective purposes.

The final, twelfth section is similarly asynchronous. Titled "Σημεῖα τοῦ λύχνου" (Sign of the Lamp), it details the vision of the "θεὸν...ἐπὶ κιβωρίου καθήμενον" (god sitting on the seed-vessel of a lotus) that is seen "μετὰ τὸ εἰπεῖν τὴν φωταγωγίαν" (after saying the evocation of light).⁷⁸ This exegesis of *PGM* IV.930–1114 now coming to an end, we may proceed to examine in greater detail the webs of connections which exist between θεαγωγία within this spell and aspects of the wider world of Graeco-Egyptian spellcraft, to yield a more nuanced and contextualized understanding of θεαγωγία itself within the papyri.

---

⁷³*LSJ*, s.v. "ἀπόλυσις."

⁷⁴*PGM*, IV.1061.

⁷⁵Ibid., IV.1065–70.

⁷⁶Ibid., IV.1071–84.

⁷⁷Ibid., IV.1085–1102. This term literally means a "fabrication" or "creation," but is given the special sense in this context in *LSJ*, s.v. "ποίησις."

⁷⁸*PGM*, IV.1102–1114.

5.3 Θεαγωγία in Later Platonism

5.3.1 Porphyry

After the aforementioned spell from the *PGM*, the next earliest attestation of θεαγωγία comes from Porphyry. In what A.R. Sodano identifies as a section of Porphyry's original *Epistula ad Anebonem*, the philosopher queries Iamblichus as to how it is that the gods "πῶς ὡς κρείττους παρακαλούμενοι ἐπιτάττονται ὡς χείρους" (while invocated as superiors, receive orders as inferiors) during the course of θεαγωγία operations.[79] While the wording is far from identical, the latter half of this quote from Porphyry preserved in Eusebius' *Praeparatio evangelica* — which questions how "διὰ νεκρῶν δὲ τὰ πολλὰ ζώων αἱ θεαγωγίαι" (live gods are evocated by means of many dead animals)[80] — is paralleled in another quote from Porphyry's *Epistula* from Iamblichus' response in *De mysteriis*. Therein, Porphyry similarly asks why it is that "διὰ δὲ νεκρῶν ζώων τὰ πολλὰ αἱ θεαγωγίαι ἐπιτελοῦνται" (many evocations of the gods are accomplished by means of dead animals).[81]

While Porphyry's objections to the practice of animal sacrifice are well recorded throughout his *De abstinentia ab esu animalium*,[82] what is different here is that he is referring to this practice occurring during the course of θεαγωγία rather than θεουργία rituals. While animal sacrifice is not at all uncommon in the spells of the magical papyri,[83] it is of great interest here that while Porphyry asks a question regarding sacrifice in θεαγωγία, Iamblichus' response to this question makes no mention of θεαγωγία. And, although he does not use this specific term either, it appears that his defense of animal sacrifice here does so in terms of theurgic

---

[79]Porphyry, *Lettera ad Anebo*, 2.8a. A fragment of the quote is preserved in Iamblichus, *On the Mysteries*, IV.1.181.

[80]Porphyry, Λεττερα αδ Ανεβο, 2.8b.

[81]Iamblichus, *On the Mysteries*, VI.1.241.

[82]Cf. Porphyry, *De l'abstinence*.

[83]One of the most picturesque instances of this can be found in *PGM* I.1–42, where a falcon is drowned in the milk of a black cow (milk which is then drunk by the operator) such that its corpse can become animated by the daemon evocated during the ritual. For this ritual in context, see: Cheak, "Waters Animating and Annihilating," 48–78. Specific instances within θεαγωγία and pḥ-nṯr spells can most clearly be seen in *PDM Suppl.* 149–62.

ritual praxis — defending animal sacrifice as a valid and proper means of offering to the gods.⁸⁴ As such, can we take this reply of Iamblichus' as an indication that he viewed θεαγωγία as identical with θεουργία (particularly with σύστασις)? As the following paragraph demonstrates, the answer to this question is a resounding *no*.

5.3.2 Iamblichus

5.3.2.1 Θεαγωγία *Contra* Θεουργία

This passage, which is Iamblichus' only other mention of θεαγωγία, implores the reader not to judge the efficacy of θεουργία by comparing it to "ἀμαθῶς ἐπιπηδώντων τῇ θεαγωγίᾳ χαρακτήριζε" (unlearned attempts at evocating the gods by symbols) performed without the correct preparation. He further decries this type of evocation as "ἀλαζονικὰ καὶ ψευδῆ" (boastful and deceitful) as compared to the "γνήσιά ... καὶ ἀληθινά" (genuine and true) θεουργία of the "ἀληθινῶν ἀθλητῶν περὶ τὸ πῦρ" (true athletes of the fire).⁸⁵

This passage is interesting in several regards. First, we see here Iamblichus making a clear dichotomy between θεαγωγία and θεουργία.⁸⁶ This bifurcation is phrased in terms of a dichotomy, whereby θεαγωγία epitomizes all that is false and θεουργία all that is true. It is also interesting to note here that the term Iamblichus uses for falsity, ἀλαζονικός, is directly related to one of the more common synonyms of γόης — ἀλαζονίας, the "magical" braggart. This tension between true θεουργία and false γοητεία was maintained by Porphyry as well, who distinguished between "ἀγύρτας καὶ ἀλαζόντας" (beggars and braggarts) and practitioners of "θεολογίας [καὶ] θεουργίας" (theology [and] theurgy).⁸⁷

So long as we can see the connection in this passage of Iamblichus' between θεαγωγία and γοητεία, the nature of his problem

---

⁸⁴Iamblichus, *On the Mysteries*, VI.1–4. For analysis of Iamblichus' attitudes toward sacrifice, see: Shaw, *Theurgy and the Soul*, 143–69; Butler, "Offering to the Gods," 1–20.

⁸⁵Iamblichus, *On the Mysteries*, II.10.92.

⁸⁶As the editors of *De mysteriis* note (ff. 147), the phrase "ἀληθινῶν ἀθλητῶν περὶ τὸ πῦρ" is synonymous with theurgists.

⁸⁷Porphyry, *Lettera ad Anebo*, 18d.1–3.

with θεαγωγία can be explained by a cross-reading from elsewhere in *De mysteriis*. In book III, he warns the reader not to equate true visions of the gods with "φαντασίαις" (images) produced by "γοητείας τεχνικῶς" (magic's artifice), as the latter are wholly lacking in truth — being "ἄχρι δὲ τοῦ δοκεῖν φαντάσματα ψιλὰ προτείνουσιν" ("mere images, reaching only as far as appearance").[88] Taking these two passages together, we arrive at a view of θεαγωγία as being concerned with the evocation of images of the gods rather than of the gods themselves.

5.3.2.2 Θεαγωγία and Impiety

Thus, we can understand this objection of Iamblichus to θεαγωγία as differentiated from those of prior philosophers. It is, in his view, not that it is merely impious to compel the gods — it is impossible. This situation wherein the gods are wholly outside the domain of even the γόης's influence is necessitated by the position of ἀνάγκη in Iamblichus' theology. He tells us that the "θεῶν ἀνάγκαι" (necessities of the gods) are not impositions placed upon them from outside parties (i.e. γόητες), but are rather "θεῶν εἰσιν ἀνάγκαι καὶ ὡς ἐπὶ θεῶν γίγνονται" (necessities of the gods, and occur by means of the nature of the gods).[89] This linguistic turnabout, "interpreting the objective genitive as a subjective gentive" serves to take the familiar idea we have seen thus far and completely turn the tables, placing the coactive power wholly in the hands of the gods rather than the γόης.[90] Hammering the point home, Iamblichus proceeds to blatantly inform his readers that the gods are "ἀκήλητον καὶ ἀπαθὲς καὶ ἀβίαστον" (unable to be enchanted, without passions, and not liable to compulsion).[91]

This position is fully borne out by what might be Iamblichus clearest statement on the subject. In *De mysteriis*'s sixth book, although he (truthfully) admits that the Egyptians sometimes issue "ἀπειλαῖς" threats to the gods — which we have seen evi-

---

[88]Iamblichus, *On the Mysteries*, III.25.160–61 (trans. Clarke, Dillon, and Hershbell).

[89]Ibid., I.14.44.

[90]Dillon, "Iamblichus' Defense of Theurgy," 35.

[91]Iamblichus, *On the Mysteries*, I.14.44.

5.3. ΘΕΑΓΩΓΙΑ IN LATER PLATONISM

denced in the magical papyri at length — that among the Chaldeans, who are the true θεουργοί, that "θεοῖς δὲ οὐδεὶς ἀπειλεῖ, οὐδ' ἐστί τις τοιοῦτος τρόπος εὐχῆς πρὸς αὐτοὺς γιγνόμενος" ("no one threatens the gods, nor does such a manner of invocation occur in relation to them").[92] While it is intensely curious that Iamblichus, who we must remember is pretending to be an Egyptian priest in this missive, would come out so strongly in favour of Chaldean as opposed to Egyptian θεουργία, we can see in this reply to Porphyry a capstone to the previous passages, noting with finality Iamblichus' conscious opposition to coactive θεαγωγία.[93]

5.3.2.3 Evocation and the Luminous Vehicle

However, as mentioned previously in the section on *PGM* IV.930–1112, the prominence of φωταγωγία in both the *PGM*'s θεαγωγία and Iamblichus' θεουργία bears some notice. Shaw treats φωταγωγία as central to Iamblichean praxis, describing the evocation of the divine light as the means through which "the soul joins god."[94] In θεουργία, this process of "φωτὸς ἀγωγὴν" (evoking the light) was seen to operate by transforming the soul's luminous vehicle into a medium through which the gods could appear.[95] In this way, just as φωταγωγία transformed the operator's lamp flame into a medium for divine manifestation in the *PGM*, so does this evocation similarly reshape the very ὄχημα of the theurgist's soul in Iamblichus' praxis. It was the case, Johnston tells us, that "the vehicle of the theurgist's soul had to be luminous before he could see the gods" which φωταγωγία becomes, as in the *PGM*, the prerequisite for any attempt at achieving σύστασις.[96]

Similarities aside, there are two important distinctions between the place of φωταγωγία in the *PGM* and in Iamblichus. First, the object being illuminated by the evoked light in the *PGM* is a material fire from a lamp, whereas in *De mysteriis* it is generally the immaterial ὄχημα. The reason for this, John-

---

[92] Ibid., VI.7.249.
[93] For more on Iamblichus' relationship with Egypt, see: Armstrong, "Iamblichus and Egypt," 179–88.
[94] Shaw, "The Role of Aesthesis in Theurgy," 99.
[95] Iamblichus, *On the Mysteries*, III.14.132.
[96] Johnston, "*Fiat lux*," 17.

ston notes, is that whereas the light entering into the soul's vehicle was guaranteed to be divine in origin, the lamplight, being manmade, "was bound to foster deception" and was prone to being hijacked by "artificial images" and "wicked demons who appear...and mislead the prophet."[97] Second, while in the *PGM*, both the φωταγωγία and θεαγωγία formulas operated by means of the practitioner imposing his will, this is not so in θεουργία. Rather, in Iamblichus' practice, it is the case that while the light is actively drawn down by the θεουργός, the divine beings which enter into his vehicle through the light do so of their own accord.[98] Thus, while the Iamblichean may engage in a coactive relationship with the transmissive light, his approach to the gods is never characterised as such.

5.3.3 Gregory of Nazianzus

While this has resolved the questions that this study set out to answer, there are yet several attestations of θεαγωγία yet to be detailed. So, in closing, I present here these post-Iamblichean instances for the sake of completion. First, in Gregory of Nazianzus' *Orationes*, we see it written that everything "ὅσα περὶ θεῶν ἢ θυσιῶν, περὶ εἰδώλων, περὶ δαιμόνων ἀγαθῶν τε καὶ κακοποιῶν, ὅσα περὶ μαντείας, θεαγωγίας, ψυχαγωγίας, ἄστρων δυνάμεως, τερατεύονται" (having to do with gods and sacrifices, with idols, with daemons whether good or evil, having to do with divination, the evocation of gods, the evocation of souls, the powers of the stars, or speaking in tongues) is nothing but nonsense.[99]

5.3.4 Basil of Seleucia

While not as dismissive as Gregory of Nazianzus, Basil of Seleucia's opinion of θεαγωγία was similarly negative; although, his objection is framed in terms which would have been familiar to Plato's contemporaries. He specifically condemned the μάγος,

---

[97]Ibid.

[98]Iamblichus, *On the Mysteries*, III.14.134. For more general information on the theology of light in Iamblichus, see: Finamore, "Iamblichus on Light and the Transparent," 55–64; Shaw, "Living Light," 59–87.

[99]Gregory of Nazianzus, *The Five Theological Orations*, I.10.

noting the "ἀνοσιουργίας" (wicked) nature of "γοητείαν τοῦ ἀνδρὸς τέχνης τὰ μιαρὰ καὶ δυσαγῆ ἀποτελέσματα, θεαγωγίας τέ τινας καὶ ψυχαγωγίας καὶ δαιμόνων ἐπικλήσεις" (man's art of goety, his theagogy and his psychagogy, his summoning of daemons).[100]

5.3.5 Proclus

In coming to Iamblichus' successor Proclus, however, we see a vastly different picture emerge. Running completely contrary to his predecessor, Proclus discusses θεαγωγία in a way that is at once distinct from both the *PGM* and Iamblichus. For, in both, θεαγωγία is viewed as a practice wherein the γόης compels the god to appear. However, in Proclus we see θεαγωγία as typical Neoplatonic invocation, where the divine manifestation is effected by sympathy rather than command.[101] He describes the theagogy as either the "θείου φωτὸς" (divine light) or "πνεῦμα θεῖον" (divine spirit) entering into a vessel once it has been purified and the obstacles blocking the god's descent have been removed.[102] This is a far cry from the conjuration of the god which culminates in the magician stepping on his feet to hold him there in the *PGM*.

5.3.6 Michael Psellus

Maintaining a more traditional attitude, Psellus describes wanting to know "τίς τε ἡ αὐτοψία ἐστι καὶ τίς ἡ θεαγωγία" (what is seeing with my own eyes and what is evocation of the gods), presuming a differentiation between truthful seeing and artificial evocation. He continues in a somewhat querulous manner, and at one point mentions the "θεοῦ πρὸς τὸν ἄνθρωπον ἀναγωγή τε καὶ κάθοδος" (evocation and descent of the gods unto man),[103] describing such things as somehow different from the divine images perceived either by the νοῦς (intellect) or the "ψυχῆς ὄχημα" (vehicle of the soul). Thus, while Psellus does seem to differentiate θεαγωγία from other activities which relate man to god, he

---

[100] Basil of Seleucia, *De vita*, I.22.10–21.
[101] Cf. Proclus, *On the Priestly Art*.
[102] Proclus' sentiments are quoted in: Psellus, *Orationes*, I.303–41.
[103] Psellus, *Theologica*, I.27.188–93.

is less than clear as to the nature of that differentiation.

The natue of θεαγωγία within Psellus' writings is a question far too great to be dealt with adequately within the confines of this section. There are many instances of it in his *Orationes* and *Theologica*. Some are commentaries on Proclus, and others are his original thoughts. Work will have to be done in the future specifically on Psellus to untangle this later phase of the history of θεαγωγία. However, at this juncture, it is worth noting that his complex ambivalence may in part be due to the heavy influence that the *Oracula Chaldaica* (alongside the writings of the Platonists themselves) had on his thought.[104]

5.3.7 Gregory Palamas

Finally, we come to the last historical attestation, found in Gregory Palamas' *Epistulae*. In a far less sophisticated manner than either Psellus or Proclus, Palamas reaches back to the late antique Church Fathers, castigating "θυσίαι, ψυχαγωγίαι τε καὶ θεαγωγίαι καὶ θεουργίαι" (sacrifices, psychagogies, theagogies, and theurgies) as "περίεργοι" (curious, or meddling) — a word whose occurrence in Acts 19:19 bears the explicit connotation of "magic."[105]

And so, our tour of the latter days of θεαγωγία is at an end. Although there is certainly a great deal of work to be done in mapping out the complex nuances and intricacies of post-Iamblichean discourses on θεαγωγία — particularly from the Church Fathers — it is my hope that this brief exploration has provided at the very least a firm foundation for this strain of research to continue.

---

[104]For more on this influence, see: Burns, "The Chaldean Oracles of Zoroaster, Hekate's Couch, and Platonic Orientalism in Psellos and Plethon," 158–79.

[105]Palamas, *Epistulae*, III.50.13. For the passage from Acts 19:19, see: *The Greek New Testament*: "ἱκανοὶ δὲ τῶν τὰ περίεργα πραξάντων συνενέγκαντες τὰς βίβλους κατέκαιον ἐνώπιον πάντων· καὶ συνεψήφισαν τὰς τιμὰς αὐτῶν καὶ εὗρον ἀργυρίου μυριάδας πέντε." *The New International Version* (*NIV*) translates this passage as: "A number who had practiced sorcery brought their scrolls together and burned them publicly. When they calculated the value of the scrolls, the total came to fifty thousand drachmas."

Chapter 6
Conclusion

In seeking to understand the historical context of θεαγωγία within the Graeco-Egyptian magical papyri, this monograph has taken the long way of getting to the goal — developing the contextual picture of θεαγωγία through prior analyses of three deeply related families of practices within the papyri: (1) binding curses, (2) erotic enchantments, and (3) necromantic and psychagogic spells. What we have seen regarding θεαγωγία, particularly its instantiations within the Graeco-Egyptian papyri, is an intriguing juxtaposition of terminologies and techniques which at once draw on sources clearly identifiable as γοητεία and others similarly identifiable as θεουργία.

On the one hand for example, the sections of *PGM* IV.930–1114 dealing with φωταγωγία bear a remarkable similarity to the way the practice is described by Iamblichus in *De mysteriis*. Its use of light as a mediating substance through which the encounter with the gods was effected bears all the hallmarks of the θεουργία of the *Oracula Chaldaica* and Iamblichus. On the other hand, the coercive elements that dominate almost every other portion of the spell are so very clearly opposed not only to the late θεουργία of Iamblichus and his followers, but to the whole prior history of γοητεία's reception by the philosophers. What, then does this tell us about the meaning of θεαγωγία within the *PGM*? At the outset of this study, I cautioned that it would be unproductive to attempt to pigeonhole θεαγωγία as being either γοητεία or θεουργία.

It should now be apparent why this is the case. Within *PGM* IV.930–1114, θεαγωγία does not appear as singularly identifiable with any such terms. It is described as operating in classificatorily ambiguous ways which defy attempts to decisively say either that "θεαγωγία is a type of γοητεία" or that "θεαγωγία is a type of θεουργία." What is undoubtable, though, is the debt owed by this ritual to both the Hellenic ἀγωγή family as well as the Demotic *pḥ-nṯr* spells. In many ways, this spell is a paragon of the syncretic Graeco-Egyptian milieu from which it emerged. On the Greek side, it draws naturally on the coercive ἐπάναγκοι with all their imperative commands and threats; and on the Egyptian side, it utilizes both the distinctively Egyptian notion of nominal coercion as well as being an evocation of Horus, an Egyptian god *par excellence*. As such, our final estimation of *PGM* IV.930–1114 must be one which views it as an extremely complex instance of several hundred years of syncretic fluctuation between various "magical" and "religious" strains of praxis — all of which resulted in a ritual which bears the fingerprints of both Greece and Egypt.

From the outset of this monograph, my aim was to explore the nature and historical context of θεαγωγία by charting its position as a member of the greater ἀγωγή family of coercive spells. While beginning from an understanding of the term on strictly linguistic grounds as a conjunction of θεός with the ἀγωγή stem, indicating something having to do with the gods and with attraction, excursions into the magical papyri quickly clarified its meaning as referring to a category of spells designed to evocate the gods to visible appearance. Its similar members within the papyri — αὔτοπτος, σύστασις, and *pḥ-nṯr*—all served to further clarify the technical details of just what a θεαγωγὸς λόγος looked like, culminating in an exegesis of the most complete instance of such a spell: *PGM* IV.930–1114.

The connections between these evocatory rituals wherein the gods were coercively called down were demonstrated to be connected in a myriad of ways to the other principle types of operations in the papyri. We saw instances of erotic ἀγωγή spells being performed by means of divine coercion, as well as necromantic ψυχαγωγία spells functioning via the same operative mechanism.

The ἀγωγή and ψυχαγωγία spells themselves also demonstrated a marked tendency to bleed into one another, with instances of erotic spells retrieving their intended victims by the intercession of ghosts being found alongside spells which are principally concerned with prophesying from the dead but can also compel the same evocated souls to coerce female victims. Both categories were also demonstrated to be inextricably linked to the early κατάδεσμοι, wherein we find the earliest instances of both erotic compulsion by "magical" means as well as coercion and binding by means of the intercession of dead souls.

The resulting image that emerges when examining θεαγωγία within this greater context of ἀγωγή, ψυχαγωγία, and the κατάδεσμοι is not one of separate strands which at times are neatly woven together. It is rather one of a knot without beginning or end — a web of interconnectivity whose members all depend on one another and are each just as tied to one member as to any other. As such, an understanding of θεαγωγία is not, and cannot be mutually exclusive of a similar understanding of the wider ἀγωγή and *ph̭-nṯr* family of coercive evocations to which it belongs.

Bibliography

Primary References

Aeschylus. *Eumenides*. In *Aeschyli septem quae supersunt tragoedias*, 247–86. Oxford: Clarendon Press, 1972.

———. *Libation Bearers*. In *Agamemnon, Libation Bearers, Eumenides, Fragments*, edited and translated by Hugh Lloyd-Jones, 155–268. Loeb Classical Library. Cambridge: Harvard University Press, 1988.

Asclepius. In *Corpus Hermeticum*, 4 vols., edited by A.D. Nock and translated by A.J. Festugière, 2:296–355. Collection des Universites de France. Paris: Les Belles Lettres, 1946–1954.

Asclepius. In *Hermetica: The Greek Corpus Hermeticum and the Latin Asclepius in a new English translation with notes and introduction*, translated by Brian P. Copenhaver, 67–92. Cambridge: Cambridge University Press, 1992.

Apollonius of Rhodes. *Apollonii Rhodii Argonautica*. Edited by H. Fraenkel. Oxford: Clarendon, 1961.

Aristophanes. *Lysistrata*. In *Birds, Lysistrata, Woman at the Thesmophoria*, edited and translated by Jeffrey Henderson, 253–442. Loeb Classical Library. London: Harvard University Press, 2000.

———. *Vespae*. In *Aristophanis fabulae*, edited by N.G. Wilson, 209–73. Oxford: Oxford University Press, 2007.

Augustine. *De civitate Dei libri xxii*. 2 vols. Edited by B. Dombart. Leipzig: Teubner, 1877.

———. *Concerning the City of God Against the Pagans*. Translated by Henry Bettenson. London: Penguin, 1984.

Basil of Seleucia. *De vita et miraculis sanctae Theclae libri ii*. In *Vie et miracles de sainte Thècle*, edited by G. Dragon, 168–412. Subsidia hagiographica 62. Brussels: Société des Bollandistes, 1978.

Cassius Dio. *Cassii Dionis Cocceiani historiarum Romanarum quae supersunt*. 3 vols. Edited by U.P. Boissevain. Berlin: Weidmann, 1895–1901.

Chaeremon of Alexandria. *Fragmenta*. In *Fragmenta historicum Graecorum*, 4 vols., edited by Karl Müller, 3: 495–99. Paris: Didot, 1841–1870.

Corpus Hermeticum. 4 vols. Edited by A.D. Nock and translated by A.J. Festugière. Collection des Universites de France. Paris: Les Belles Lettres, 1946–1954.

Corpus Hermeticum. In *Hermetica: The Greek Corpus Hermeticum and the Latin Asclepius in a new English translation with notes and introduction*, translated by Brian P. Copenhaver, 1–66. Cambridge: Cambridge University Press, 1992.

Crowley, Aleister. *Magick in Theory and Practice*. In *Magick: Book Four, Parts I–IV*, edited by Hymenaeus Beta, 2nd edition, 119–286. York Beach: Samuel Weiser, 2000.

Curse Tablets and Binding Spells from the Ancient World. Edited by John G. Gager. Oxford: Oxford University Press, 1992.

Defixionum tabellae. Edited by Augustus Audollent. Paris: Fontemoing, 1904.

Defixionum tabellae Atticae. Edited by Richard Wünsch. Corpus inscriptionum Atticarum. Berlin: Georgium Reimerum, 1897.

Eusebius. *Eusebii Pamphili: Evangelicae preparationis libri xv*. Translated by E.H. Gifford. Oxford: E Typographeo Academico 1903.

———. *Eusebius Werke VIII: Die Praeparatio Evangelica*. Edited by Karl Mras. Die Griechischen Christlichen Schriftseller der Ersten Jahrhunderte 43.1. Berlin: Akademie-Verlag, 1954.

Gorgias. *Fragmenta.* In *Die Fragmente der Vorsokratiker*, 3 vols., edited by H. Diels and W. Kranz, 6th edition, 2: 279–306. Berlin: Weidmann, 1952.

———. "The Encomium of Helen." In *The Greek Sophists*, translated by John Dillon and Tania Gergel, 76–84. London: Penguin, 2003.

Gregory of Nazianzus. *The Five Theological Orations of Gregory of Nazianzus.* Edited by Arthur James Mason. Cambridge Patristic Texts. Cambridge: At the University Press, 1899.

Heraclitus. *Fragmenta,* In *Die Fragmente der Vorsokratiker*, 3 vols., edited by H. Diels and W. Kranz, 6th edition, 1: 150–82. Berlin: Weidmann, 1952.

Hermias. *Hermiae Alexandri in Platonis Phaedrum scholia.* Edited by P. Couvreur. Paris: Librairie Émile Bouillon, 1901.

Hesiod. *Works and Days.* In *Hesiod, Homeric Hymns, Epic Cycle, Homerica*, edited and translated by Hugh G. Evelyn-White, 2–63. Loeb Classical Library. Cambridge: Harvard University Press, 1995.

Homer. *The Iliad.* 2 vols. Edited and translated by A.T. Murray. Loeb Classical Library. London: William Heinemann, 1928.

———. *The Odyssey.* 2 vols. Edited and translated by A.T. Murray. Loeb Classical Library. London: William Heinemann 1919.

Iamblichus. *On the Mysteries: Translated with Introduction and Notes.* Edited and translated by Emma C. Clarke, John M. Dillon, and Jackson P. Hershbell. Writings from the Greco-Roman World 4. Atlanta: Society of Biblical Literature, 2003.

Julian. *Fragments of a Letter to a Priest.* In *The Works of the Emperor Julian*, 3 vols., edited and translated by Wilmer Cave Wright, 2: 297–344. Loeb Classical Library. London: William Heinemann, 1913.

Livy. *History of Rome.* 14 vols. Edited and translated by B.O. Foster. Loeb Classical Library. London: William Heinemann, 1919–1959.

Nonnus. *Dionysiaca*. 3 vols. Edited and translated by W.H.D. Rouse. Loeb Classical Library. London: William Heinemann 1940–1942.

Orphei hymni. Edited by W. Quandt. 3rd edition. Berlin: Weidmann, 1962.

Ostraka. In *Papyri Graecae magicae: Die Griechischen Zauberpapyri*, 2 vols., edited and translated by Karl Preisendanz, 2: 209–11. Leipzig: Teubner, 1928–1931.

Ovid. *Metamorphoses: Recognovit breviqve adnotatione critica instrvxit*. Edited by R.J. Tarrant. Oxford Classical Texts. Oxford: Oxford University Press, 2004.

———. *The Amores*. In *Heroides and Amores*, edited and translated by Grant Showerman, 313–508. Loeb Classical Library. London: William Heinemann, 1914.

Palamas, Gregory. *Epistulae*. In *Γρηγορίου τοῦ Παλαμᾶ συγγράμματα*, 8 vols., edited by Panagiotis P. Chrestou, 203–312. Thessalonique, 1962.

Papyri Graecae magicae: Die Griechischen Zauberpapyri. 2 vols. Edited and translated by Karl Preisendanz. Leipzig: Teubner, 1928–1931.

Pherecydes of Athens. "Pherekydes of Athens (*Fragments 1–89*)," edited and translated by William S. Morison. In *Brill's New Jacoby*, edited by Ian Worthington. Leiden: Brill, 2013.

Pindar. *The Pythian Odes*. In *The Odes of Pindar: Including the Principal Fragments*, edited and translated by John Sandys, 151–312. Loeb Classical Library. London: William Heinemann, 1915.

Plato. *Gorgias*. In *Platonis opera*, edited by John Burnet, 5 vols., 3:447–527. Oxford Classical Texts. Oxford: Clarendon Press, 1900–1907.

———. *Gorgias*, translated by Donald J. Zeyl. In *Complete Works*, edited by John M. Cooper, 791–869. Indianapolis: Hacket, 1997.

———. *Leges*. In *Platonis opera*, edited by John Burnet, 5 vols., 5: 624–969. Oxford Classical Texts. Oxford: Clarendon Press, 1900–1907.

———. *Laws*, translated by Trevor J. Sauders. In *Complete Works*, edited by John M. Cooper, 1318–1616. Indianapolis: Hacket, 1997.

———. *Respvblica*. In *Platonis opera*, 5 vols., edited by John Burnet, 4:327–621. Oxford Classical Texts. Oxford: Clarendon Press, 1900–1907.

———. *Republic*, trans. by G.M.A. Grube and C.D.C. Reeve. In *Complete Works*, edited by John M. Cooper, 971–1223. Indianapolis: Hacket, 1997.

———. *Symposium*. In *Platonis opera*, 5 vols., edited by John Burnet, 2:172–223. Oxford Classical Texts. Oxford: Clarendon Press, 1900–1907.

———. *Symposium*, translated by Alexander Nehamas and Paul Woodruff. In *Complete Works*, edited by John M. Cooper, 457–505. Indianapolis: Hacket, 1997.

Plotinus. *Enneads*. 6 vols. Edited and translated by A.H. Armstrong. Loeb Classical Library. London: William Heinemann, 1966–1988.

Plutarch. *Aristides*. In *Lives*, 11 vols., edited and translated by Bernadotte Perrin. Loeb Classical Library. London: William Heinemann, 1914–1926.

———. *De defectu oraculorum*. In *Plutarchi moralia*, 6 vols., edited by Kurt Hubert and others, 3rd edition, 3: 59–122. Leipzig: Teubner, 2013.

———. *De Iside et Osiride*. In *Plutarchi moralia*, 6 vols., edited by Kurt Hubert and others, 3rd edition, 2.3:1–80. Leipzig: Teubner, 2013.

Porphyry. *De l'abstinence*. 3 vols. Edited by Jean Bouffartigue, Michel Patillon, and Alain Seconds. Collection des universités de France. Paris: Belles Lettres, 1977.

———. *On Abstinence from Killing Animals*. Translated by Gillian Clark. Ithaca: Cornell University Press, 2000.

———. *Porfirio: Lettera ad Anebo*, Edited by A.R. Sodano. Naples: L'Arte Tipografica, 1958.

Proclus. *De sacrificio et magia.* In *Catalogue des manuscrits alchemiques grecs*, 8 vols., edited by J. Bidez, 6:148–51. Brussels: Lamertin, 1928.

———. *In Platonis Timaeum Commentarii*, 3 vols., edited by E. Diehl. Leipzig: Teubner, 1903–1906.

———. *On the Priestly Art According to the Greeks*, translated by Brian P. Copenhaver. In *Hermeticism and the Renaissance: Intellectual History and the Occult in Early Modern Europe*, edited by Ingrid Merkel and Allen G. Debus, 79–110. Washington: Folger Books, 1988.

———. *Procli Diadochi in Platonis rem publicam commentarii.* 2 vols. Edited by W. Kroll. Leipzig: Teubner, 1899–1901.

Psellus, Michael. *Michaelis Pselli theologica: vol. I.* Edited by P. Gautier. Leipzig: Teubner, 1989.

———. *Orationes forensis et acta.* Edited by G.T. Dennis. Bibliotheca scriptorum Graecorum et Romanorum Teubneriana. Stuttgart: Teubner, 1994.

Sappho. *Sappho: Text.* In *Greek Lyric I: Sappho and Alcaeus*, edited and translated by David A. Campbell, 52–205. Loeb Classical Library. Cambridge: Harvard University Press, 1982.

Sophocles. *Fragmenta.* In *Tragicorum Graecorum fragmenta*, 5 vols., edited by Bruno Snell and others, 99–656. Göttingen: Vandenhoeck & Ruprecht, 1971–2004.

Sudiae lexicon. 4 vols. Edited by A. Adler. Lexicographi Graeci. Leipzig: Teubner, 1928–1935.

Supplementum magicum. 2 vols. Edited by Robert Walter Daniel and Franco Maltomini. Papyrologica Coloniensia 16.1–2. Opladen: Westdeutscher Verlag, 1990–1992.

The Chaldean Oracles: Text, Translation, and Commentary. Edited and translated by Ruth Majercik. 2nd edition. Platonic Texts and Translations 8. Wiltshire: The Prometheus Trust, 2013.

The Demotic Magical Papyrus of London and Leiden. 3 vols. Edited by F.L. Griffith and Herbert Thompson. London: H. Grevel, 1904–9.

The Derveni Papyrus. Edited by Theokritos Kourmenos and others. Studi e Testi per il Corpus Dei Papiri Filosofici Greci e Latini 13. Firenzi: Leo S. Olschki, 2006.

The Greek Magical Papyri in Translation, Including the Demotic Spells. Edited by Hans Dieter Betz, translated by Hans Dieter Betz and others. Chicago: The University of Chicago Press, 1986.

The Greek New Testament: SBL Edition. Edited by Michael W. Holmes. Atlanta: Society of Biblical Literature, 2010.

The Holy Bible, New International Version. Grand Rapids: Zondervan Publishing House, 1984.

The Sacred Disease. In *Hippocrates: With an English Translation*, 10 vols., edited and translated by W.H.S. Jones, 2:127–84. Loeb Classical Library. London: William Heinemann, 2012.

Theodoret of Cyrus. *Graecarum affectionum curatio*. In *Théodoret de Cyr: Thérapeutique des maladies helléniques*, 2 vols., edited by P. Canivet, 2:296–446. Sources chrétiennes 57. Paris: Éditions du Cerf, 1958.

Theodosius II. *Theodosiani libri xvi*. Edited by Theodor Mommsen and Paul M. Meyer. Berlin: Weismannos, 1905.

Valerius Flaccus. *Argonautica*. Edited and translated by J.H. Mozley. Loeb Classical Library. Cambridge: Harvard University Press, 1934.

Zosimus of Panopolis. Περὶ ὀργάνων καὶ καμίνων γνήσια ὑπομνήματα περὶ τοῦ ω στοιχείου. In *Les alchimistes grecs: Tome IV*, edited by Michèle Mertens, 1–10. Paris: Les Belles Lettres, 1995.

Secondary References

A Greek-English Lexicon. Edited by Henry George Liddell and Robert Scott, revised by Henry Stuart Jones and Roderick McKenzie. Oxford: Clarendon Press, 1996.

Addey, Crystal. "Divine Possession and Divination in the Graeco-Roman World: The Evidence from Iamblichus' *On the Mysteries*." In *Spirit Possession and Trance: New Interdisciplinary Perspectives*, edited by Bettina Schmidt and Lucy Huskinson, 171–85. Continuum Advances in Religious Studies. London: Continuum International, 2010.

———. "Divine Possession and Divination in the Graeco-Roman World: The Evidence from Iamblichus' *On the Mysteries*." In *Spirit Possession and Trance: New Interdisciplinary Perspectives*, edited by Bettina Schmidt and Lucy Huskinson, 171–85. Continuum Advances in Religious Studies. London: Continuum International, 2010.

———. "Oracles, Dreams and Astrology in Iamblichus' *De mysteriis*." In *Seeing with Different Eyes: Essays in Astrology and Divination*, edited by Patrick Curry and Angela Voss, 35–58. Newcastle upon Tyne: Cambridge Scholars, 2007.

Armstrong, A.H. "Iamblichus and Egypt." *Les Études philosophiques* 2/3 (1987): 179–88.

———. "Was Plotinus a Magician?" *Phronesis* 1, no. 1 (1975): 73–79.

Audollent, Augustus. "Prooemium." In *Defixionum tabellae*, edited by Augustus Audollent, xvii–cxxviii. Paris: Fontemoing, 1904.

Athanassiadi, Polymnia. "Dreams, Theurgy and Freelance Divination: The Testimony of Iamblichus." *The Journal of Roman Studies* 83 (1993): 115–30.

———. *Mutations of Hellenism in Late Antiquity*. Variorum Collected Studies Series. London: Routledge, 2016.

———. "The Chaldean Oracles: Theology and Theurgy." In *Pagan Monotheism in Late Antiquity*, edited by Polymnia Athanassiadi and Michael Frede, 149–84. Oxford: Clarendon Press, 1999.

Bailey, Michael D. "The Meanings of Magic." *Magic, Ritual, and Witchcraft* 1, no. 1 (2006): 1–23.

Bassett, Samuel E. "ΔΑΙΜΩΝ in Homer." *The Classical Review* 33, no. 7/8 (1919): 134–6.

Betz, Hans Dieter. "Introduction" and "Commentary." In *The "Mithras Liturgy": Text, Translation, and Commentary*, 1–38, 60–226. Tübingen: Mohr Siebech, 2003.

———. "List of Papyri in Preisendanz." In *The Greek Magical Papyri in Translation, Including the Demotic Spells*, xxiii–xxv. Chicago: The University of Chicago Press, 1986.

———. "Magic and Mystery in the Greek Magical Papyri." In *Magika Heira: Ancient Greek Magic and Religion*, edited by Christopher A. Faraone and Dirk Obbink, 244–59. Oxford: Oxford University Press, 1991.

———. "The Formation of Authoritative Tradition in the Greek Magical Papyri." In *Hellenisms und Urchristentum*, edited by Hans Dieter Betz, 173–83. Tübingen: J.C.B. Mohr, 1990.

———. *The "Mithras Liturgy": Text, Translation, and Commentary*. Studien und Texte zu Antike und Christentum, 18 (Tübingen: Mohr Siebeck 2003).

Bremmer, Jan N. "The Birth of the Term 'Magic.'" In *The Metamorphosis of Magic from Late Antiquity to the Early Modern Period*, edited by Jan N. Bremmer and Jan R. Veenstra, 1–11. Groningen Studies in Cultural Change 1. Leuven: Peeters, 2002.

Broadie, Sarah. *Nature and Divinity in Plato's Timaeus*. Cambridge: Cambridge University Press, 2012.

Burkert, Walter. *Greek Religion*. Translated by John Raffan. Cambridge: Harvard University Press, 1985.

Burns, Dylan. "The Chaldean Oracles of Zoroaster, Hekate's Couch, and Platonic Orientalism in Psellos and Plethon." *Aries: Journal for the Study of Western Esotericism* 6, no. 2 (2006): 158–79.

Butler, Edward P. "Offering to the Gods: A Neoplatonic Perspective." *Magic, Ritual, and Witchcraft* 2, no. 1 (2007): 1–20.

Buxton, R.G.A. *Persuasion in Greek Tragedy: A Study of Peitho*. Cambridge: Cambridge University Press, 1982.

Ciraolo, Leda Jean. "Supernatural Assistants in the Greek Magical Papyri." In *Ancient Magic and Ritual Power*, edited by Marvin W. Meyer and Paul Allan Mirecki, 279–95. Religions in the Graeco-Roman World 129. Leiden: Brill, 1995.

Clark, Stephen R.L. "Plotinus: Charms and Countercharms." *Royal Institute of Philosophy Supplement* 65 (2009): 215–31.

Clarke, Emma C. *Iamblichus' De mysteriis: A Manifesto of the Miraculous*. Ashgate New Critical Thinking in Theology and Biblical Studies. Aldershot: Ashgate, 2001.

Clarke, Emma C., John M. Dillon and Jackson P. Hershbell. "Introduction." In *On the Mysteries: Translated with Introduction and Notes*, xiii–lii. Writings from the Greco-Roman World 4. Atlanta: Society of Biblical Literature, 2003.

Collins, Derek. *Magic in the Ancient Greek World*. Blackwell Ancient Religions. Oxford: Blackwell, 2008.

Copenhaver, Brian P. "Introduction." In *Hermetica: The Greek Corpus Hermeticum and the Latin Asclepius in a new English translation with notes and introduction*, translated by Brian P. Copenhaver, xiii–lxi. Cambridge: Cambridge University Press, 1992.

Cornford, Francis MacDonald. *Plato's Cosmology: The Timaeus of Plato Translated with a Running Commentary*. The International Library of Philosophy. London: Routledge, 2001.

Dickie, Matthew W. *Magic and Magicians in the Greco-Roman World*. London: Routledge, 2001.

Dielman, Jacco. *Priests, Tongues, and Rites: The London-Leiden Magical Manuscripts and Translation in Egyptian Ritual (100–300 CE)*. Religions in the Graeco-Roman World 153. Leiden: Brill, 2005.

———. "Scribal Practices in the Production of Magic Handbooks in Egypt." In *Continuity and Innovation in the Magical Tradition*, edited by Gideon Bohak and others, 85–118. Jerusalem Studies in Religion and Culture 15. Leiden: Brill, 2011.

Dietrich, Albrecht. *Eine Mithrasliturgie*. Leipzig and Berlin: Teubner, 1910.

Dictionnaire Grec-Français: composé sur un nouveau plan. Edited by Charles Alexandre. Paris: Libraire de L. Hachette, 1859.

Dillon, John M. "Iamblichus' Defense of Theurgy: Some Reflections." *The International Journal of the Platonic Tradition* 1 (2007): 30–41.

———. *The Middle Platonists: 80 B.C. to A.D. 220.* Ithaca: Cornell University Press, 1996.

Dodds, E.R. "Theurgy and Its Relationship to Neoplatonism." *The Journal of Roman Studies* 37, no. 1/2 (1947): 55–69.

Dodson, Derek S. *Reading Dreams: An Audience-Critical Approach to the Dreams in the Gospel of Matthew.* Library of New Testament Studies. London: T&T Clark International, 2009.

Durkheim, Emile. *The Elementary Forms of the Religious Life.* Translated by Joseph Ward Swain. London: George Allen & Unwin, 1915.

Eitrem, Samson. "Dreams and Divination in Magical Ritual," translated by Dirk Obbink. In *Magika Heira: Ancient Greek Magic and Religion*, edited by Christopher A. Faraone and Dirk Obbink, 175–87. Oxford: Oxford University Press, 1991.

Evans-Grubbs, Judith. "Abduction Marriage in Antiquity: A Law of Constantine (*CTh* IX.24.1) and its Social Context." *The Journal of Roman Studies* 79 (1989): 59–83.

Fairbanks, Arthur. "The Chthonic Gods of Greek Religion." *The American Journal of Philology* 21, no. 3 (1900): 241–259.

Faraone, Christopher A. *Ancient Greek Love Magic.* Cambridge: Harvard University Press, 1999.

———. "Necromancy Goes Underground: The Disguise of Skull- and Corpse-Divination in the Paris Magical Papyri (*PGM* IV 1928–2144)." In *Mantikê: Studies in Ancient Divination*, edited by Sarah Iles Johnston and Peter T. Struck, 255–82. Religions in the Graeco-Roman World 155. Leiden: Brill, 2005.

———. "The Agonistic Context of Early Greek Binding Spells." In *Magika Heira: Ancient Greek Magic and Religion*, edited by Christopher A. Faraone and Dirk Obbink, 3–32. Oxford: Oxford University Press, 1991.

Finamore, John F. *Iamblichus and the Theory of the Vehicle of the Soul.* American Classical Studies 14. Chico: Scholars Press, 1985.

———. "Iamblichus on Light and the Transparent." In *The Divine Iamblichus: Philosopher and Man of the Gods*, edited by H.J. Blumenthal and E.G. Clark, 55–64. London: Bristol Classical Press, 1993.

Fowden, Garth. *The Egyptian Hermes: A Historical Approach to the Late Pagan Mind.* Mythos. Princeton: Princeton University Press, 1993.

Fraser, Kyle A. "The Contested Boundaries of 'Magic' and 'Religion' in Late Pagan Monotheism." *Magic, Ritual, and Witchcraft* 4, no. 2 (2009): pp. 131–51.

Frazer, James George. *The Golden Bough: A Study in Magic and Religion.* Abridged edition. New York: Touchstone, 1996.

Gager, John R. "Introduction." In *Curse Tablets and Binding Spells from the Ancient World*, edited by John R. Gager, 3–41. Oxford: Oxford University Press, 1992.

———. "Sex, Love, and Marriage." In *Curse Tablets and Binding Spells from the Ancient World*, edited by John R. Gager, 78–85. Oxford: Oxford University Press, 1992.

Graf, Fritz. *Magic in the Ancient World.* Translated by Franklin Philip. Revealing Antiquity 10. Cambridge: Harvard University Press, 2008.

———. "Prayer in Magic and Religious Ritual." In *Magika Heira: Ancient Greek Magic and Religion*, edited by Christopher A. Faraone and Dirk Obbink, 188–97. Oxford: Oxford University Press, 1991.

Haluszka, Adria. "Sacred Signified: The Semiotics of Statues in the Greek Magical Papyri." *Arethusa* 41, no. 3 (2008): 479–94.

Hammond, Dorothy. "Magic: A Problem in Semantics." *American Anthropologist* 72, no. 6 (1970): 1349–56.

Hanegraaff, Wouter J. *Esotericism and the Academy: Rejected Knowledge in Western Culture*. Cambridge: Cambridge University Press, 2012.

Helleman, Wendy Elgersma. "Plotinus and Magic." *The International Journal of the Platonic Tradition* 4 (2010): 114–46.

Johnson, Janet H. "Louvre E 3229: A Demotic Magical Text." *Enchoria* 8 (1977): 55–102.

Johnston, Sarah Iles. *Ancient Greek Divination*. Blackwell Ancient Religions. Oxford: Blackwell, 2008.

———. "Animating Statues: A Case Study in Ritual." *Arethusa* 41, no. 3 (2008): 445–77.

———. "Crossroads." *Zeitschrift für Papyrologie und Epigraphik* 88 (1991): 217–24.

———. "*Fiat lux, fiat ritus*: Divine Light and the Late Antique Defense of Ritual." In *The Presence of Light: Divine Radiance and Religious Experience*, edited by Matthew T. Kapstein, 5–24. Chicago: University of Chicago Press, 2004.

———, *Hekate Soteira: A Study of Hekate's Role in the Chaldean Oracles and Related Literature*. American Classical Studies 21. Atlanta: Scholars Press, 1990.

———. "*Homo fictor deorum est*: Envisioning the Divine in Late Antique Divinatory Spells." In *The Gods of Ancient Greece: Identities and Transformations*, edited by Jan N. Bremmer and Andrew Erskine, 406–21. Edinburgh Leventis Studies 5. Edinburgh: Edinburgh University Press, 2010.

———. "Magic and the Dead in Classical Greece." In *Greek Magic: Ancient, Medieval and Modern*, edited by J.C.B. Petropoulos, 14–20. London: Routledge, 2008.

———. *Restless Dead: Encounters Between the Living and the Dead in Ancient Greece*. Berkeley: University of California Press, 1999.

Jordan, D.R. "A Survey of Greek Defixiones Not Included in the Special Corpora." *Greek, Roman, and Byzantine Studies* 26, no. 2 (1985): 151–97.

———. "New Greek Curse Tablets (1985–2000)." *Greek, Roman, and Byzantine Studies* 41 (2000): 5–46.

Kagarow, Eugen G. *Griechische Fluchtafeln*. Eus Supplementa 4. Leopoli: Societatem philologam polonorum, 1929.

Kenyon, Frederic G. *The Palaeography of Greek Papyri*. Oxford: Clarendon Press, 1899.

Kissling, Robert Christian. "The Οχημα-Πνευμα of the Neo-Platonists and the De Insomniis of Synesius of Cyrene." *The American Journal of Philology* 43, no. 4 (1922): 318–30.

Krulak, Todd C. "The Animated Statue and the Ascension of the Soul: Ritual and Divine Image in Late Platonism." PhD dissertation, University of Pennsylvania, 2009.

Lenormant, François. *Catalogue d'une collections d'antiquités Égyptiennes*. Paris: Maulde et Renou, 1857.

Lewy, Hans. *Chaldaean Oracles and Theurgy: Mysticism, Magic and Platonism in the Later Roman Empire*. 3rd edition. Edited by Michel Tardieu, Série Antiquité 77. Paris: Institut d'Études Augustiniennes, 2011.

Lexico de magia y religión en los papiros mágicos griegos. Edited by L. Muñoz Delgado and J. Ródriguez Somolinos. Diccionario Griego-Español 5. Madrid: CSIC, 2001.

Lindsay, Jack. *The Origins of Alchemy in Graeco-Roman Egypt*. New York: Barnes and Noble, 1970.

Love, Edward O.D. *Code-Switching with the Gods: The Bilingual (Old Coptic-Greek) Spells of PGM IV (P. Bibliothèque Nationale Supplément Grec. 574) and their Linguistic, Religious, and Socio-Cultural Context in Late Roman Egypt*. Zeitschrift für ägyptische Sprache und Altertumskunde 4. Berlin: Walter de Gruyter, 2016.

Lycourinos, Damon Zacharias. *Ritual Embodiment in Modern Western Magic: Becoming the Magician*. Gnostica. Oxon: Routledge, 2018.

———. "The Spell of Pnouthis as a Mystery Rite in the Greek Magical Papyri." In *Occult Traditions*, edited by Damon Zacharias Lycourinos, 19–32. Numen, 2012.

———. "Those Who Wander in the Night: Magoi Amongst the Hellenes." In *Kratos: The Hellenic Tradition*, edited by Gwendolyn Taunton, 55–74. Melbourne: Numen Books, 2013.

Majercik, Ruth. "Introduction." In *The Chaldean Oracles: Text, Translation, and Commentary*, edited and translated by Ruth Majercik, 2nd edition, 1–46. Platonic Texts and Translations 8. Wiltshire: The Prometheus Trust, 2013.

Malinowski, Bronislaw. "Magic, Science, and Religion." In *Magic, Science and Religion and Other Essays*, edited by Robert Redfield, 1–71. Glencoe: The Free Press, 1948.

Marx-Wolf, Heidi. "High Priests of the Highest God: Third-Century Platonists as Ritual Experts." *Journal of Early Christian Studies* 18, no. 4 (2010): 481–513.

Merlan, Philip. "Plotinus and Magic." *Isis* 44, no. 4 (1953): 341–48.

Mohr, Richard D. *The Platonic Cosmology*. Philosophia Antiqua 42. Leiden: Brill, 1985.

Moyer, Ian. "Thessalos of Tralles and Cultural Exchange." In *Prayer, Magic, and the Stars in the Ancient and Late Antique World*, edited by Scott Noegel and others, 39–56. Magic in History. University Park: The Pennsylvania State University Press, 2003.

Normand, Claudine. "System, Arbitrariness, Value." In *The Cambridge Companion to Saussure*, edited by Carol Sanders, 88–106. Cambridge: Cambridge University Press, 2004.

Nyord, Rune. *Breathing Flesh: Conceptions of the Body in Ancient Egyptian Coffin Texts*. CNI Publications 37. Copenhagen: CNI Publications, 2009.

Ogden, Daniel. *Greek and Roman Necromancy*. Princeton: Princeton University Press, 2001.

———. *Magic, Witchcraft, and Ghosts in the Greek and Roman Worlds: A Sourcebook*. Oxford: Oxford University Press, 2002.

Pachoumi, Eleni. "Divine Epiphanies of Paredroi in the Greek Magical Papyri." *Greek, Roman, and Byzantine Studies* 51 (2011): 155–65.

———. *The Concepts of the Divine in the Greek Magical Papyri*. Studien und Texte zu Antike und Christentum 102. Tübingen: Mohr Siebeck, 2017.

Plaisance, Christopher A. "Occult Spheres, Planes, and Dimensions: Geometric Terminology and Analogy in Modern Esoteric Discourse." *Journal of Religious History* 40, no. 3 (2016): 385–404.

———. "Of Cosmocrators and Cosmic Gods: The Place of the Archons in *De mysteriis*." In *Daimonic Imagination: Uncanny Intelligences*, edited by Angela Voss and William Rowlandson, 64–85. Newcastle upon Tyne: Cambridge Scholars, 2013.

———. "The Transvaluation of 'Soul' and 'Spirit': Platonism and Paulism in H.P. Blavatsky's *Isis Unveiled*." *Pomegranate: The International Journal of Pagan Studies* 15, no. 1 (2013): 250–72.

Renberg, Gil H. *Where Dreams May Come: Incubation Sanctuaries in the Greco-Roman World*. Religions in the Graeco-Roman World 184. Leiden: Brill, 2017.

Ritner, Robert Kriech. "Egyptian Magical Practice Under the Roman Empire: The Demotic Spells and Their Religious Context." *Aufstieg und Niedergang der römischen Welt* II.18.5 (1995): 3333–79.

———. *The Mechanics of Ancient Egyptian Magical Practice*. Studies in Ancient Oriental Civilization 54. Chicago: The Oriental Institute of the University of Chicago, 1993.

Rubio, Gonzalo. "The Inventions of Sumerian: Literature and the Artifacts of Identity." In *Problems of Canonicity and Identity Formation in Ancient Egypt and Mesopotamia*, edited by Kim Ryholt and Gojko Barjamovic, 231–258. The Carsten Niebuhr Publication Series 43. Copenhagen: CNI Publications, 2016.

Segal, Alan. "Hellenistic Magic: Some Questions of Definition." In *Studies in Gnosticism and Hellenistic Religions: Presented* to *Gilles Quispel on the Occasion of His 65th Birthday*, edited by R. van den Broek and Maarten J. Vermaseren, 349–75. Education and Society in the Middle Ages and Renaissance. Leiden: Brill, 1982.

Schibli, H.S. "Hierocles of Alexandria and the Vehicle of the Soul." *Hermes* 121 (1993): 109–17.

Schreckenberg, Heinz. *Ananke: Untersuchungen zur Geschichte des Wortgebrauchs*. Zetemata 36. Munich: C.H. Beck, 1964.

Shaw, Gregory. "After Aporia: Theurgy in Later Platonism." In *Gnosticism and Later Platonism: Themes, Figures, and Texts*, edited by John D. Turner and Ruth Majercik, 57–82. Symposium Series 12. Atlanta: Society of Biblical Literature, 2000.

———. "Living Light: Divine Embodiment in Western Philosophy." In *Seeing with Different Eyes: Essays in Astrology and Divination*, edited by Patrick Curry and Angela Voss, 59–87. Newcastle upon Tyne: Cambridge Scholars, 2007.

———. "The Role of Aesthesis in Theurgy." In *Iamblichus and the Foundations of Late Platonism*, edited by Eugene Afonasin and others, 91–112. Ancient Mediterranean and Medieval Texts and Contexts 13. Leiden: Brill, 2012.

———. "Theurgy: Rituals of Unification in the Neoplatonism of Iamblichus." *Traditio* 41 (1985): 1–28.

———. *Theurgy and the Soul: The Neoplatonism of Iamblichus*. Hermeneutics: Studies in the History of Religions. University Park: The Pennsylvania State University Press, 1995.

Smith, Andrew. *Porphyry's Place in the Neoplatonic Tradition: A Study in Post-Plotinian Neoplatonism*. The Hague: Martinus Nijhoff, 1974.

Tambiah, Stanley Jeyaraja. "Form and Meaning of Magical Acts: A Point of View." In *Modes of Thought: Essays on Thinking in Western and Non-Western Societies*, edited by Robin Horton and Ruth Finnegan, 199–229. London: Faber, 1973.

Tanaseanu-Döbler, Ilinca. *Theurgy in Late Antiquity: The Invention of a Ritual Tradition*. Beiträge zur Europäischen Religionsgeschichte 1. Göttingen: Vandenhoeck & Ruprecht, 2013.

The Demotic Dictionary of the Oriental Institute of the University of Chicago. Edited by Janet H. Johnson. Chicago: The Oriental Institute of the University of Chicago, 2002.

Thorndike, Lynn. *A History of Magic and Experimental Science.* 8 vols. New York: Columbia University Press, 1923–1958.

Tylor, Edward B. *Primitive Culture: Researches Into the Development of Mythology, Philosophy, Religion, Language, Art, and Custom.* 2 vols. London: John Murray, 1920.

Van Bladel, Kevin. *The Arabic Hermes: From Pagan Sage to Prophet of Science.* Oxford Studies in Late Antiquity. Oxford: Oxford University Press, 2009.

Van den Berg, R.M. *Proclus' Commentary on the Cratylus in Context: Ancient Theories of Language and Naming.* Philosophia Antiqua 112. Leiden: Brill, 2008.

Van den Broek, Roelof. "Gnosticism and Hermetism in Antiquity: Two Roads to Salvation." In *Gnosis and Hermeticism: From Antiquity to Modern Times*, edited by Roelof van den Broek and Wouter J. Hanegraaff, 1–20. SUNY Series in Western Esoteric Traditions. Albany: State University of New York Press, 1998.

———. "The Creation of Adam's Psychic Body in the Apocryphon of John." In *Studies in Gnosticism and Hellenistic Religions: Presented to Gilles Quispel on the Occasion of His 65th Birthday*, edited by Roelof van den Broek and Maarten Jozef Vermaseren, 38–57. Leiden: Brill, 1981.

Versnel, H.S. "Beyond Cursing: The Appeal to Justice in Judicial Prayers." In *Magika Heira: Ancient Greek Magic and Religion*, edited by Christopher A. Faraone and Dirk Obbink, 60–106. Oxford: Oxford University Press, 1991.

Voss, Angela. "The Secret Life of Statues." In *Sky and Psyche: The Relationship Between Cosmos and Consciousness*, edited by Nicholas Campion and Patrick Curry, 201–28. Edinburgh: Floris, 2006.

Winkler, John J. "The Constraints of Eros." in *Magika Heira: Ancient Greek Magic and Religion*, edited by Christopher A. Faraone and Dirk Obbink, 214–43. Oxford: Oxford University Press, 1991.

Woodard, Roger D. "Introduction." In *The Ancient Languages of Mesapotamia, Egypt and Aksum*, edited by Roger D. Woodard, 1–18. Cambridge: Cambridge University Press, 2008.

Index Locorum

AESCHYLUS
  Choephori
    937ff, 63
  Eumenides
    306, 27
    332, 27
APOLLONIUS OF RHODES
  Argonautica
    3.840, 38
ARISTOPHANES
  Lysistrata
    599–601, 62
  Vespae
    804, 38
ASCLEPIUS
  24, 18
AUGUSTINE
  De civitate Dei
    X.9.10–11, 20
    X.9.18, 20
    X.9.18–19, 20

BASIL OF SELEUCIA
  De vita et miraculis sanctae Theclae libri ii
    I.22.10–21, 2, 97

CASSIUS DIO
  Historiarum Romanarum quae supersunt
    L.5.1, 30
    L.5.3–4, 30
CHAEREMON OF ALEXANDRIA
  Fragmenta
    fr. 3, 11
CORPUS HERMETICUM
  I.24–26, 19
  XVII.8–13, 18

DE MORBO SACRO
  I.2.1–10, 14
  I.4.1–21, 14
DEFIXIONUM TABELLAE
  52.14–16, 33
  67, 34
DEFIXIONUM TABELLAE ATTICAE
  55a.16–17, 29
  87a, 33
  77, 50

EUNAPIUS
  Vitae sophistarum
    368–73, 17
    434–5, 18
EUSEBIUS
  Praeparatio evangelica
    III.16.2, 38
    IV.23.6, 38
    V.10.1–3, 2, 10

FLACCUS
  Argonautica
    7.147ff, 63

GORGIAS
  Fragmenta
    fr. 10, 14

GREGORY OF NAZIANZUS
  Orationes
    I.10, 2, 96

HERACLITUS
  Fragmenta
    fr. 14, 13

HERMIAS OF ALEXANDRIA
  In Platonis Phaedrum scholia
    87.5–13, 18

HESIOD
  Opera et dies
    122–23, 36
  Theogonia
    913–14, 46

HOMER
  Ilias
    I.222, 36
    III.420, 36
  Odyssea
    11.568ff, 63
    X.203–43, 7
    XI.90–149, 7

HYMNI HOMERICI
    II.431, 46

IAMBLICHUS
  De mysteriis
    I.14, 55
    I.14.44, 94
    II.10.92, 2, 93

    II.4.75, 88
    III.14.132, 95
    III.14.133, 88
    III.14.134, 96
    III.25.160, 22
    III.25.160–61, 94
    III.31.176, 88
    IV.1.181, 92
    IX.9.284, 82
    V.23.233–34, 18
    VI.1–4, 93
    VI.1.241, 2, 10, 92
    VI.7.249, 95
    VIII.5, 67
    X.6, 19

JULIAN THE APOSTATE
  Epistulae
    293a–294c, 18

LIVY
  Ab urbe condita libri
    I.9–13, 46

LOUVRE E 3229
    55–102, 12
    6.11, 80
    6.13–16, 80
    6.6, 80
    6.7–10, 80
    90, 77

MARINUS OF NEAPOLIS
  Vita Procli sive de felicitate
    13.320–3, 16
    26.624–6, 16

NONNUS
  Dionysiaca
    II.108ff, 66

NOVUM TESTAMENTUM GRAECE

Acts 19:19, 98

ORACULA CHALDAICA
  fr. 110, 18
  fr. 120, 19
  fr. 121, 19
  fr. 122, 19
  fr. 136, 18
  fr. 153, 16
  fr. 196, 18
  fr. 208, 17, 85
  fr. 224, 18
ORPHEI HYMNI
  1.3, 38
  56.8–11, 57
OSTRAKA
  1.6, 58
OVID
  Amores
    III.7.27–30, 28
  Metamorphoses
    I.689ff, 66

PALAMAS, GREGORY
  Epistulae
    III.50.13, 2, 98
PAPYRI DEMOTICAE MAGICAE
  LXI, 12
  XII, 12
  XIV, 12
  xiv.117–49, 80
  xiv.150–231, 80, 86
  xiv.232–38, 80
  xiv.459–75, 86
  xiv.475–88, 86
  xiv.489–515, 86
  xiv.516–27, 86
  xiv.805–40, 80
  xiv.93–114, 81

PAPYRI GRAECAE MAGICAE
  930–1114, 80
  I.1–42, 69, 92
  I.127, 22
  I.305, 58
  I.306, 58
  I.308, 58
  I.310, 58
  I.312, 58
  I.342, 58
  I.42–195, 79
  I.53–54, 22
  II.45, 90
  III.197, 17, 83
  III.229, 58
  III.391, 58
  III.393, 58
  III.394, 58
  III.48, 58
  III.494, 17, 83
  III.71, 58
  III.90, 58
  IV, 11
  IV.1002, 89
  IV.1007, 89
  IV.1015, 89
  IV.1019, 89
  IV.1023–4, 89
  IV.1035, 90
  IV.1036, 89
  IV.1036–37, 89
  IV.1038–46, 90
  IV.1046–52, 90
  IV.1051–56, 90
  IV.1057, 90
  IV.1061, 91
  IV.1065–70, 91
  IV.1071–84, 91

INDEX LOCORUM

IV.1085–1102, 91
IV.1102–1114, 91
IV.1390–1495, 44, 62
IV.1394, 62
IV.1398–1434, 62
IV.1412–13, 62
IV.1433, 62
IV.1443–55, 63
IV.1456–57, 63
IV.1459–68, 63
IV.1496–1595, 48
IV.1509–10, 48, 52
IV.1510–22, 48
IV.1527–31, 48
IV.1531–3, 49
IV.1541, 48
IV.1551, 58
IV.1557, 58
IV.1708, 58
IV.1716–1870, 29, 50
IV.1721, 50
IV.1722, 51
IV.1722–37, 51
IV.1737–43, 51
IV.1743–8, 51
IV.1748–1833, 51
IV.1928, 66
IV.1928–2005, 69, 72
IV.1933–34, 69
IV.1948–49, 69
IV.1967–68, 69
IV.1971–72, 69
IV.2006, 70
IV.2006–2125, 70–76
IV.2014–31, 70
IV.2031, 72
IV.2031–34, 70
IV.2034–53, 70

IV.2054–60, 70
IV.2060–61, 71
IV.2061, 72
IV.2064–65, 71
IV.2065–72, 71
IV.2072–74, 71
IV.2076–78, 73
IV.2081, 67
IV.2088–91, 73
IV.2140, 66, 67
IV.2140–44, 67, 69
IV.2312, 58
IV.2441–2621, 49, 56
IV.2441–44, 56
IV.2567–68, 56
IV.2573, 56
IV.2679–80, 56
IV.2708–84, 63
IV.2714ff, 65
IV.2730, 65
IV.2731–33, 65
IV.2735–44, 65
IV.289, 58
IV.2891–2942, 57, 58, 71
IV.2891–92, 57
IV.2901, 57
IV.2903, 57
IV.2904, 57
IV.2912–14, 57
IV.2915, 57
IV.2938–39, 58
IV.296–303, 53
IV.296–466, 29, 49, 51, 52, 72
IV.3018, 58
IV.3033, 58
IV.3037, 58
IV.3039, 58

IV.304–21, 53
IV.3045, 58
IV.3058, 58
IV.3062, 58
IV.3065, 58
IV.3075, 58
IV.3078, 58
IV.3081, 58
IV.3112, 90
IV.3205, 58
IV.321–30, 53
IV.332–4, 53
IV.336–350, 52
IV.345, 58
IV.351–53, 52
IV.361, 58, 72
IV.368, 72
IV.395–406, 52
IV.396, 58
IV.397, 72
IV.475–829, 19, 87
IV.537–57, 19
IV.538, 87
IV.779, 17, 83
IV.930, 17, 83
IV.930–1112, 2, 95
IV.930–1113, 8
IV.930–1114, 3, 80, 82, 83, 85, 87, 88, 90, 91, 99, 100
IV.930–54, 85
IV.949–53, 85
IV.950, 85
IV.956–57, 87
IV.959–60, 86
IV.970, 88
IV.973–85, 87
IV.974–75, 2

IV.977, 58, 87
IV.978, 58
IV.978–80, 87
IV.985–87, 2
IV.986–87, 89
IV.987–88, 89
LI.1, 72
LI.21, 72
LI.5, 72
LVII.1–37, 69
LXI.39–44, 44
LXXXIV, 30
V.334, 72
V.370–421, 18
V.370–446, 74
V.370–90, 74
V.390–97, 74
V.418, 74
V.419, 75
V.435–9, 75
V.440–6, 75
V.54–69, 68, 83
Va.1–3, 83
VI.1, 17, 83
VI.39, 17, 83
VII.1006, 72
VII.242, 58
VII.243, 58
VII.246, 58
VII.319–34, 83
VII.335–47, 83
VII.396–404, 28
VII.407–10, 74
VII.462–66, 29
VII.540–78, 86
VII.593–619, 44
VII.727–39, 83
VII.993–1009, 72

VIII.1–63, 51
XII.14–95, 29, 69
XII.491, 72
XII.84, 58
XIII.278, 58
XIII.734, 85
XIVa.1–11, 81
XIVa.4, 81
XIVa.5, 81
XIVa.7–9, 81
XIXa, 30
XIXa.15, 72
XV.1, 41
XV.10, 41
XV.13, 41
XV.16, 41
XV.2, 41
XV.4–5, 41
XV.5, 41
XV.8, 41
XVI, 30
XVI.1, 72
XVI.17, 58
XXXVI.153, 58
XXXVI.250, 58
XXXVI.258, 58
PAPYRUS DERVENI
 VI.2–4, 40
PDM SUPPLEMENTUM
 149–62, 80, 92
 162–68, 80
PHERECYDES OF ATHENS
 Fragmenta
  1–89, 30
PINDAR
 Pythia
  IV.213–19, 45
  IV.218, 45, 51

  IV.291, 45
PLATO
 Gorgias
  523a, 63
 Leges
  909b, 40
  933a–b, 14, 27, 29
 Respvblica
  364b–c, 15
 Symposium
  202e, 37
PLOTINUS
 Enneades
  IV.4.40.1, 31
  IV.4.40.1–6, 31
  IV.4.40.19, 31
PLUTARCH
 Aristides
  21, 62
 De defectu oraculorum
  416c–d, 37
 De Iside et Osiride
  361b–c, 38
PORPHYRY
 Epistula ad Anebonem
  18d.1–3, 20, 93
  2.8a, 92
  2.8a–b, 10
  2.8b, 92
PROCLUS
 De sacrificio et magia
  148–51, 18
 In Platonis rem publicam commentarii
  II.11.18, 17, 85
 In Platonis Timaeum commentarii
  fr. 2, 18

fr. 20, 18
PSELLUS, MICHAEL
  Orationes forensis et acta
    I.303–41, 2, 97
  Pselli theologica
    I.27.188–93, 2, 97

SAPPHO
  Fragmenta
    1.18–9, 44
SOPHOCLES
  Fragmenta
    fr. 535.2, 38
SUDIAE LEXICON
  s.v. γοητεία, 22, 40
SUPPLEMENTUM MAGICUM
  24.fr.a.1, 58
  29.8, 58
  38.8, 51
  39.1, 72
  46.5, 58
  47.14, 72
  47.18, 72
  48.14, 72
  48J.20, 72
  48J.31, 72
  48J.6, 72
  49.28, 72
  49.33, 72
  49.48, 58
  50.12, 72
  50.48, 58
  54.30, 58
  57.1, 58, 72

THEODORET OF CYRUS
  Graecarum affectionum curatio
    III.66–67, 11

THEODOSIUS II
  Codex Theodosianus
    IX.24.1, 47

ZOSIMUS OF PANOPOLIS
  De littera Omega
    1–10, 67
    75–6, 67

Index Nominum

Aïdoneus, 46
Addey, Crystal, 11, 17, 75, 83
Adonis, 57
Aeschylus, 27, 63
Alexandre, Charles, 9
Antonius, Marcus, 30
Apollonius of Rhodes, 38
Aristophanes, 38
Armstrong, A.H., 31, 95
Athanassiadi, Polymnia, 15, 75
Audollent, Augustus, 26, 31
Augustine, 20

Bailey, Michael, 4
Basil of Seleucia, 2, 96–97
Bassett, Samuel E, 36
Betz, Hans Dieter, 6, 11, 12, 19, 22, 41, 50, 79, 87
Bidez, Joseph, 70
Bitys, 66, 67
Bremmer, Jan N., 7, 12
Broadie, Sarah, 37
Burkert, Walter, 36
Burns, Dylan, 13, 98
Butler, Edward P., 93
Buxton, R.G.A., 44

Cassius Dio, 30
Chaeremon of Alexandria, 11
Cheak, Aaron, 92

Ciraolo, Leda Jean, 69
Circe, 7, 8
Clark, Stephen R.L., 31
Clarke, Emma C., 11, 88
Cleopatra, 30, 31
Collins, Derek, 7, 8, 12–14, 26, 28, 29, 40, 43
Constantine, 47
Copenhaver, Brian P., 68
Cornford, Francis MacDonald, 37
Crowley, Aleister, 1
Cumont, Franz, 70

Dardanos, 50
De Saussure, Ferdinand, 10
Dickie, Matthew W., 6–8, 12, 13, 26–28, 30
Dielman, Jacco, 12, 17, 77
Dieterich, Albrecht, 11
Dillon, John M., 11, 15, 37, 82, 94
Diomata, 37
Dodds, E.R., 15, 20
Dodson, Derek S., 74
Durkheim, Émile, 5

Eitrem, Samson, 74
Empedocles, 37
Eunapius, 17, 18

129

Eusebius, 2, 10, 38, 92
Evans-Grubbs, Judith, 47

Fairbanks, Arthur, 35
Faraone, Christopher A., 6, 25–29, 32–35, 43–50, 52, 53, 61
Finamore, John F., 19, 96
Flaccus, 63
Fowden, Garth, 67, 68, 78, 79
Fraser, Kyle, 9
Frazer, James George, 5, 34

Gager, John R., 6, 27–33, 35, 36, 50
Gorgias, 13, 14
Graf, Fritz, 4, 6, 8, 12, 13, 26–29, 32–34, 89
Gregory of Nazianzus, 2, 96
Grese, W.C., 67, 83
Griffith, F.L., 77

Haluszka, Adria, 18
Hammond, Dorothy, 4
Hanegraaff, Wouter J., 4, 13
Helen of Troy, 36
Helleman, Wendy Elgersma, 31
Heraclitus, 12, 13
Hermes Trismegistus, 67
Hermias of Alexandria, 18
Hershbell, Jackson P., 11
Hesiod, 36, 37, 46
Hippocrates, 14
Homer, 7, 8, 36, 63, 66

Iamblichus, 2, 3, 8, 10, 16–20, 50, 55, 67, 81, 86, 88, 92–99

Jason, 45, 51

Johnson, Janet H., 77
Johnston, Sarah Iles, 13–16, 18–20, 38, 40, 61, 62, 83, 86, 87, 95, 96
Jordan, D.R., 25–28, 36
Julian the Apostate, 18
Julian the Chaldean, 15
Julian the Theurgist, 15

Kagarow, Eugen G., 32, 35
Kenyon, Frederic, 11
Kissling, Robert Christian, 19
Krulak, Todd C., 17, 75

Lenormant, François, 11
Lewy, Hans, 9, 15, 18
Liddell, Henry George, 9
Lindsay, Jack, 70
Livy, 46
Love, Edward O.D., 79
Lycourinos, Damon Zacharias, 13, 19, 22

Majercik, Ruth, 15–17, 19, 85
Malinowski, Bronislaw, 5
Marinus of Neapolis, 15
Marx-Wolf, Heidi, 15
Maximus of Ephesus, 18
Medea, 45, 51
Merlan, Philip, 31
Mohr, Richard D., 37
Moyer, Ian, 78

Nonnus, 66
Normand, Claudine, 10
Nyord, Rune, 34

O'Neil, E.N, 83
O'Neil, E.N., 48, 53
Odysseus, 7, 8

INDEX NOMINUM

Ogden, Daniel, 4, 14, 15, 27, 28, 50, 66, 68
Ostanes, 70
Ovid, 28, 29, 66

Pachoumi, Eleni, 56, 69, 71
Palamas, Gregory, 2, 98
Pherecydes of Athens, 30
Pindar, 45–46, 51
Pitys, 66–76
Plato, 14, 15, 27, 29, 37, 40, 63, 67, 96
Plotinus, 16, 31
Plutarch, 37
Porphyry, 2, 10, 11, 20, 92–93, 95
Preisendanz, Karl, 41, 83
Proclus, 2, 17, 18, 79, 85, 97–98
Psellus, Michael, 2, 97–98

Renberg, Gil H., 74
Ritner, Robert Kriech, 17, 78, 79
Romulus, 46
Rubio, Gonzalo, 35

Sappho, 44–45
Schibli, H.S., 19
Schreckenberg, Heinz, 55
Scott, Robert, 9
Segal, Alan, 6
Shaw, Gregory, 15, 16, 20, 93, 95, 96
Smith, Andrew, 11
Sodano, Angelo, 10, 92
Sophocles, 38
Syrianus, 18

Tambiah, Stanley Jeyaraja, 34
Tanaseanu-Döbler, Ilinca, 15, 16

Theodoret of Cyrus, 11
Theodosius II, 47
Thompson, Herbert, 77
Thorndike, Lynn, 5
Tiresias, 7
Tylor, Edward, 4

van Bladel, Kevin, 70
Van den Berg, R.M., 79
van den Broek, Roelof, 41, 68
Versnel, H.S., 33, 35, 36
Voss, Angela, 18

Wünsch, Richard, 26
Winkler, John J., 25, 29, 44, 50, 51, 55, 74
Woodard, Roger D., 35

Xenocrates, 37

Zosimus of Panopolis, 67

Index Rerum

Adjuration, 58–59
Alchemy, 70
Amulet, 91
Analogy, 28, 80
Angels, 1, 69, 79
    Archangels, 81, 82
Animal Sacrifice, 92–93
Anteros, 17
Archons
    Hebdomadic, 41
Ass, 70
Assistant (Magical), 69
Atheism, 14
Athens, 38
Attendants, 63

Barbarous Names, 35, 48, 53, 57, 67, 70, 74, 75, 79, 85
Begging, 13–15, 20
Bibliothèque Nationale, 11
Binding Tablets, 27
Breath, 51
Bridal Theft, 46–49
Burned Offerings, 57

Carnivores, 63
Cemetery, 28, 62, 69
Circle (Magical), 1, 70
Classical Studies, 5

Coercion, 26
Compulsion, 25, 40, 42, 44, 55–59, 65, 69, 71, 78–80, 94–96, 99, 100
Contract, 71
Divine, 42, 78
Erotic, 73
Language, 32–34, 63, 65, 71, 74, 75, 90, 91, 100
Oaths, 58–59
Cosmos, 79
Crossroads, 27, 38
Cumin, 63
Curse Tablets, 26, 27, 42
    Classification, 31–35
    Creators, 30–31
    Materials, 27–30
    Popularity, 26–27
    Terminological Legalism, 33–34

Daemons, 1, 17, 33, 35–40, 42, 43, 63, 69, 70, 79, 81, 82, 96, 97
Benevolent, 22
Chthonic, 52, 73
Classification, 36
Darkness, 88
Dead, 70–73

INDEX RERUM

Erinyes, 35
Eros, 17
Etymology, 36
Jovian, 82
Malicious, 38
Moirai, 63
Nymphs, 66
Obstructing, 40
Poine, 63
Dead, 33, 36, 62, 70
   and Daemons, 38–40
   Animals, 92
   Animation, 72
   Childless, 41
   Corpse, 67, 68, 70
   Corpses, 63
   Ghosts, 61, 63, 79, 101
   Gladiators, 62
   Heroes, 62
   Manes, 36
   Place, 69
   Reanimation, 68, 70, 73
   Soul, 69, 71
   Souls, 37, 42, 62, 63, 65, 66, 69, 70, 72, 101
   Spirit, 69
   Unmarried, 41
   Untimely, 36, 53, 65
   Violent, 53, 69
Death, 35
Deception, 14, 30
Divination, 96
Divine Epiphany, 17
Doorways, 27, 38
Dreams, 63
   Divination, 73–75
   Sending, 73–75
Drugs, 8

Earth, 38
Essence, 29
Evocation, 1, 3, 17, 42–44, 49, 62, 63, 68–73
   Darkness, 87–88
   Divine, 43, 70, 73, 75–101
   Light, 86–87, 95–96
   Souls, 96
   Theory, 81–82

Fire, 95
   Athletes, 93
Flax, 67
Funerary Lament, 13, 40

Gnosticism, 68
Goat Fat, 63
Gods, 1, 2, 9, 10, 12, 14–17, 19, 20, 22, 26, 33, 36, 37, 40, 42, 43, 45, 55, 58, 59, 65, 66, 70, 72, 77–79, 81, 94–97, 99, 100
   Adonis, 57
   Aeacus, 63
   Anubis, 63
   Aphrodite, 17, 36, 44, 45, 51, 53, 57–59, 71
   Apollo, 83
   Ares, 53
   Artemis, 63
   Chaos, 63
   Chthonic, 28, 35, 52, 63, 72
   Chthonic Hermes, 33
   Cytheria, 57
   Darkness-Bringing, 87
   Demeter, 35, 46
   Demeter Malophoros, 27
   Erebos, 63
   Ereshkigal, 35, 65

Eros, 51
Gaia, 35
Hades, 35, 46, 57
Harpocrates, 82, 89
Hecate, 18, 35, 38–40, 62, 63, 65
Helios, 69
Helios Mithras Aion, 20
Hermes, 35, 63, 74, 75
Horus, 82, 89–91, 100
Horus-Amon, 79
Iao, 35, 41, 90
Images, 94
Jupiter, 82
Kore, 35, 63
Osiris, 35
Pan, 66
Peitho, 44, 45, 51
Persephone, 35, 46, 65
Planetary, 19
Pluto, 35, 63
Psyche, 51
Sabaoth, 41
Selene, 38, 63
Selene Hecate, 56
Size, 88
Solar, 87
Suconaioi, 34
Sulis, 35
Syria, 34
Thoth, 67, 80
Underworld, 63, 65
Visible, 19
Golden Age, 36
Graveyards, 27
Great Magical Papyrus of Paris, 10, 11

Handmaidens, 63

Hermetism, 67, 68
Heroes, 65
Hide, 70
Homology, 80
Hydromancy, 80
Hymn, 85
Hymns, 69

Idols, 96
Illness, 73
Images, 97
Initiation Rituals, 13, 22
Insomnia, 65
Intellect, 97
Invocation, 1, 3, 17, 18, 40, 62, 72, 85, 86, 89, 92, 95, 97

Juggling, 13

Knowledge, 14, 68, 69
    Divine, 68

Light, 97, 99
Liminality, 38
Lotus, 91
Lychnomancy, 80, 86, 91, 95

Macrocosm, 1
Magic, 1, 3
    Formula, 9
    Homeopathic, 34
    Importance of Names, 79
    Methodological Problems, 3–9
    Persuasive Analogy, 34
    Sympathetic, 34
    Terminology, 12–23
Medicine, 76
Mediums, 17

INDEX RERUM   135

Metaphysics, 25
Methodology
    Essentialism, 4–5
    Linguisticism, 4–9, 25
    Philology, 5
Microcosm, 1
Monotheism, 9
Moon, 38, 40, 88
Musée gréco-romain d'Alexandrie, 41
Myrrh, 48
Mystery Rites, 13

Necessity, 71, 94
Nymphs, 35

Oaths, 63
Occultism, 3
Oracles, 68, 78, 80

Palaeography, 11
Papyrus, 71
Persuasion, 22, 44
Phantasms, 94
Philosophers, 2, 14, 76, 99
Philosophy, 94
Phylactary, 91
Piety, 2, 13–15, 20, 94–95
Platonic Form, 4
Platonism, 37, 79, 98
    Cosmology, 37
    Middle Platonism, 16, 18, 19, 36–38, 40
    Neoplatonism, 11, 15–20, 97
    Platonic Philosophers, 15
Possession, 83
Priests, 13
Prophecy, 68
Psychagogy, 61–76

Punishment, 71
Purification, 19, 20
Pyromancy, 80

Quackery, 14, 20

Religion, 4–6, 8, 9, 16
    Gnosticism, 41
    Mithraism, 19

Sabine Women, 46
Sacrifices, 37, 62, 96, 98
Science, 4–6
Scribal Compilation, 11
Scribes, 30
Seers, 14, 15
Sins, 13, 63
Skull, 68
Sleep, 65
Social Sciences, 4
    Sociology, 47
Soul, 13, 19, 20, 50, 68, 69
    Dead, 69
    Hateful, 40
    Luminous Vehicle, 19, 95–97
Spells
    Antagonistic, 73
    Binding, 15, 25–42, 49–59, 68, 72, 73, 79, 99, 101
    Bringing, 9
    Curse, 13
    Erotic, 9, 25, 43–59, 61–66, 68–70, 72–76, 83, 99, 100
    Evocation, 9, 10, 12
    Exorcism, 13
    Illumination, 10
    Invocation, 22
    Love Charm, 9

Necromantic, 8, 10, 43, 61–76, 99, 101
Prayer, 45
Religious, 3
Spirit, 51
Divine, 97
Spirits, 1, 63
Sun, 88
Intelligible, 38
Supplication, 33, 65
Symbols, 93
Syncretism, 78, 79, 100
Syria, 17

Theology, 20, 35–36, 94
Egyptian, 79, 94
Thessaly, 66, 67
Theurgy, 15–22, 92–101
Ascension, 19–20, 87
Conjunction, 16–17
Statue Animation, 17–18
Threats, 94, 95
Torture, 62
Triangle (Magical), 1

Underworld, 35, 46, 57, 63, 68

Vengeance, 63
Visions, 94

Will, 96

Index Verborum Demoticorum

nṯr, 77

pḥ, 77
pḥ-nṯr, 3, 12, 17, 77–81, 85, 92, 100, 101
pḫr, 78, 79

wꜥ, 80
wḥe, 77
wḥe-nṯr, 77

Index Verborum Graecorum

ἀβίαστος, 94
ἀγαθοποιός, 22
ἀγαθός, 96
ἄγαμος, 41
ἄγγελος, 69
ἅγιος, 69, 70
ἁγνός, 37
ἄγνυμι, 48
ἀγύναιοί, 65
ἀγύρτης, 14, 20, 93
ἄγω, 9, 43, 44, 48, 50, 52, 55, 56, 62, 63, 71, 73
ἀγωγεύς, 63
ἀγωγή, 3, 9, 10, 12, 25, 31, 35, 42–50, 52, 55–59, 61–63, 65–76, 79, 81, 83, 95, 100, 101
Ἄδωνις, 57
ἀεί, 81
ἀθλητής, 93
Αἰακός, 63
Ἀΐδης, 57
αἰδώς, 45
αἴω, 90
αἰών, 52
ἄκραντος, 19
ἀκήλητος, 94
ἄκρος, 15
ἀκτίς, 87
ἀλαζονίας, 14, 20, 93
ἀλαζονικός, 2, 93
ἀλεξίκακος, 36
ἀλήθεια, 69
ἀληθής, 2
ἀληθινός, 20, 93
ἀλκή, 87
ἄλλος, 52
ἀμαθής, 2, 93
ἁμάρτημα, 13
ἁμαρτία, 63
Ἄμμων, 79
ἀμφίπολος, 63
ἀνάγκη, 55–58, 71, 79, 94
ἀνάγω, 22, 40
ἀναγωγή, 10, 16, 19, 87
ἀνάκρισις, 67, 69
ἀναπέμπω, 63
ἀνασπάω, 87
ἄνασσα, 38
ἀνέρχομαι, 57
ἀνήρ, 52, 97
ἄνθρωπος, 37, 41, 97
ἀνοσιουργίας, 97
ἀοιδή, 45

ἀόρατος, 86
ἀπαθής, 94
ἄπαις, 41, 65
ἀπαραίτητος, 70
ἄπας, 52
ἀπειλέω, 95
ἀπειλή, 94
ἀποθνήσκω, 65
ἀποκρύπτω, 88
Ἀπόλλων, 83
ἀπόλυσις, 90, 91
ἀποτελέσματα, 97
ἀπόφθεγμα, 65
ἀργύριον, 98
ἀρετή, 15
Ἄρης, 53
ἁρπάζω, 46
Ἁρποκράτης, 89
ἀρχάγγελος, 81
ἄρχων, 38
ἀστήρ, 57
ἄστρον, 96
αὐγή, 87, 91
αὐτοπτέω, 83
αὐτοπτικός, 83
αὔτοπτος, 80, 82, 83, 85, 86, 100
αὐτοψία, 85
αὐτοψία, 97
ἀφαιρέω, 45, 65
Ἀφροδίτη, 57
ἄχρι, 94
ἀωΐ, 90
ἄωροι, 36
ἄωρος, 53, 65

βαίνω, 46
βάκχοις, 12
βασανίζω, 62
βασιλεύς, 68

βασκανία, 63
βιαιοθάνατος, 69
βίαιος, 53, 62
Βίτυς, 66
βοηθός, 69
βραδύς, 89
βύβλος, 98

γόος, 13, 40
γεννήτορα, 86
γῆ, 46
γίγνομαι, 87, 94, 95
γνησιά, 93
γνήσιος, 2
γνῶσις, 68
γοητεύω, 14
γόης, 13, 15, 20, 22, 30, 31, 33, 34, 36, 40–42, 44, 47–53, 56–59, 61–63, 65, 66, 68, 69, 71–74, 86, 93, 94, 97
γοητεία, 8, 13–16, 20, 22, 31, 40, 42, 50, 78, 93, 94, 97, 99, 100
γοητεύω, 40
γόνυ, 53
γράφω, 71

δαιμόνιον, 88
δαίμων, 22, 36–38, 40, 41, 63, 69, 73, 81, 96, 97
Δάρδανος, 50
δείκνυμι, 87
δεῖνα, 63
δέσμιος, 27
δεσμός, 57
δεύτερος, 81
δέω, 57
διαφέρω, 22

δίδωμι, 69
διορκίζω, 41
δισσός, 13
δοκέω, 94
δουλόω, 30
δύναμαι, 14
δύναμις, 96
δυνάστης, 89
δυσαγῆ, 97

εἶδος, 4
ἐγοήτευσε, 30
εἴδωλον, 63, 96
εἱμαρτὴν, 16
εἰμί, 94
εἰσέρχομαι, 75, 87, 89, 90
Ἑκάτη, 38, 62, 65
ἔκδικος, 69
ἐμμένω, 48
ἐμπέλασις, 19
ἐμποδών, 40
ἐμφανῆναι, 74
ἔμψυχός, 18
ἐνέργεια, 22
ἐνίοτε, 87, 88
ἐνόδιος, 38
ἐνπνευμάτωσον, 87
ἐνώπιος, 98
ἐξορκίζω, 41, 70, 71, 81, 90
ἐπαγωγή, 14, 31
ἐπαναγκαστικός, 56
ἐπάναγκος, 56, 57, 59, 62, 75, 89, 100
ἐπαοιδή, 45
ἐπαρίστερα, 34
ἐπίθυμα, 57
ἐπιθύω, 48
ἐπικαλέομαι, 89
ἐπικαλέω, 89

ἐπικλάω, 97
ἐπίκλησις, 22
ἐπιλαμπόντων, 88
ἐπιλοίμια, 14, 40
ἐπιπηδώντων, 93
ἐπιτάσσω, 90
ἐπιτάττονται, 92
ἐπιτελοῦνται, 92
ἐπῳδή, 45
ἐράω, 52
Ἑρμῆς, 33, 74
ἔρχομαι, 48
ἐσθλός, 36
εὑρίσκω, 98
εὐχή, 95
ἔνεροι, 38
ἐχθρός, 40

ζήω, 90, 92
ζῷον, 92

ἡδονή, 52
ἥλιος, 88
ἥρως, 62, 65

θαυμαστός, 51, 52
θεά, 22
θεαγωγέω, 9
θεαγωγία, 1–4, 8–12, 17, 25, 35, 42–44, 49, 55, 58, 61, 66, 68, 70, 72, 74, 75, 77–82, 85–87, 89, 91–101
θεαγωγός, 9, 16, 20, 55, 68, 89, 95, 100
θεῖος, 97
θεῖος, 87
θέλημα, 49
θεολογία, 20, 93

θεοπαράδοτα, 15
θεός, 9, 10, 20, 22, 36, 37, 41,
    52, 55, 63, 70, 81, 89–
    91, 94–97, 100
θεουργία, 2–4, 9, 15, 16, 20, 22,
    67, 74, 75, 83, 86, 92,
    93, 95, 96, 98–100
θεουργικάς, 15
θεουργός, 17–19, 22, 85, 96
θεά, 57
θεραπευτής, 20
θεοσεβής, 14
Θεσσαλός, 67
θνητός, 37
θύρα, 38
θυσία, 96, 98

Ἰάω, 90
ἱερατικός, 22, 71
ἱερός, 22, 87, 91
ἱκανός, 98
ἰσχυρός, 70
ἴωα, 90

καθαρθέντες, 38
κάθημαι, 53, 91
κάθοδος, 97
καθοπλίζω, 53
καίω, 48
κακοποιός, 96
κακός, 88
καλέω, 65, 81, 87
Καλλίας, 32
καταγράφω, 33
κατάδεσις, 14
κατάδεσμος, 14, 25–36, 40–43,
    48, 50–52, 55, 56, 58,
    61, 62, 66, 67, 73, 75,
    101

καταδέω, 26, 30, 34, 41, 50, 52
κατακαίω, 98
κατακλίνω, 56, 73
καταλέγω, 69
καταχθόνιος, 73
κατεξουσιάζω, 69
κατέχω, 33, 69, 73
κάτοχος, 87, 90
κηρός, 29
κιβώριον, 91
Κίττος, 32
κλίνω, 50
κολάζω, 37
κόλασις, 71
κόλλημα, 71
κρατέω, 53
κρείσσων, 92
Κυθήρια, 57
Κυπρογενής, 57
κυρία, 62
κύριος, 89, 90

λαμβάνω, 88
λέγω, 91
λεπτός, 19
λήναις, 12
λίθος, 50
λίσσομαι, 45
λιτή, 45
λίτομαι, 45
λόγος, 9, 55, 56, 73, 83, 87, 89,
    100
λυχνομαντεία, 86
λύχνος, 91

μαγγανάριος, 14
μαγγανεία, 30
μαγεία, 7, 8, 12, 13, 15, 16, 22,
    31, 78

μαγεύω, 14
μαγνητικός, 50
μάγοις, 12
μάγος, 12–15, 20, 22, 30, 31, 36, 40, 42, 67, 96
Μανία, 33
μαντεία, 96
μαντεῖον, 68
μάντις, 14
μαντοσύνη, 75
μάστιξ, 45
μέγας, 81, 89, 90
μεταξύ, 37
μήτηρ, 46
μιαρός, 97
μικρός, 16
μόλυβδος, 29
μονομάχος, 62
μυριάς, 98
μύσταις, 12
μυστήριον, 16

νεκρομαντεία, 68
νεκρός, 40, 92
νεκυδαίμων, 70–73
νέκυς, 38, 63, 68, 69
νόος, 97
νυκτιπόλος, 12
νύξ, 74

ξίφος, 50, 53

οἶδα, 14
ὅλος, 88
ὀνειραιτησία, 74
ὀνειραιτητέω, 73
ὀνειροπομπέω, 56
ὀνειροπομπεία, 74
ὀνειροπομπέω, 73

ὄνειρος, 63, 74
ὄνομα, 70
ὀπάων, 63
ὀπισθάγγωνα, 53
ὁράω, 57, 74
ὁρκίζω, 41, 57–59, 71, 87
ὅρκος, 58, 63
οὐδείς, 95
οὐρανός, 41, 88
οὐσία, 29
ὄχημα, 19, 95, 97
ὄψις, 22

πάθος, 37
πανταχοῦ, 38
παραγίγνομαι, 71
παρακαλέω, 92
παραμένω, 87
πᾶς, 98
πείθω, 22, 44
πέντε, 98
περίεργος, 98
Πίτυς, 66–68, 70
πιχαρουρ, 79
πλάσμα, 74
πλέως, 14
πνεῦμα, 63, 69, 87, 97
πνέω, 50, 51
ποθέω, 52
ποιέω, 49
ποίησις, 91
Ποινή, 63
πολύς, 92
πονηρός, 38
πορεύω, 63
πρᾶξις, 57, 91
πράσσω, 98
προσδοκάω, 71
προτείνω, 94

προφήτης, 67
πῦρ, 19, 87, 93
πυρομαντεία, 86
πως, 89, 92

ῥῆμα, 34

σελήνη, 88
σημεῖον, 91
σκῆνος, 67
σκοτία, 87
σκότος, 88
σκύφος, 68
σμύρνα, 48
συμφέρω, 98
συμψηφίζω, 98
συνεργός, 88
σύστασις, 16, 17, 80, 83, 85, 93, 95, 100
σφάζω, 62
σφόδρα, 14
Σωσιμένεος, 32

τάξις, 81
τάχος, 62
ταχύς, 56
τελεστική, 16–19, 75
τελέω, 58
τερατεύονται, 96
τέχνη, 13, 97
τεχνικός, 22, 94
τιμή, 98
τοκεύς, 45
τόπος, 41
τρόπος, 95

ὑπερέχω, 81
ὕπνος, 74
ὕψιστος, 81

φαίνω, 74, 89, 90
φαντασίαις, 94
φαντασία, 22
φάντασμα, 94
φάος, 86–88, 95, 97
φαρμακεία, 8
φάρμακον, 8
φέρω, 46
φιλέω, 49, 51, 52
φιλοῦσάν, 52
φιλτροκατάδεσμος, 51–53, 55, 72
φίλτρον, 51, 52
φράζω, 69
φρήν, 27
φυλακτήριον, 91
φύλαξ, 36, 37
φωταγωγέω, 10
φωταγωγία, 10, 86–88, 91, 95, 96, 99
φωταγωγός, 88

χαιρετισμός, 90
χαρακτηρίζω, 93
χείρων, 92
χθόνιος, 33, 38, 52
χρημάτισον, 75
χρόνος, 52
χωρέω, 91
χῶρος, 69

ψευδής, 2, 93
ψιλός, 94
ψυχαγωγία, 7, 9, 10, 35, 40, 61, 62, 65–73, 75, 81, 96–98, 100, 101
ψυχή, 13, 19, 38, 40, 50, 63, 97
ψυχρός, 34
ψωμίον, 62

ωαϊ, 90

ὠμοφάγος, 63
Ὧρος, 89
ὥσπερ, 88

Index Verborum Latinorum

acus, 28
anima, 20

carmen, 28
cera, 28
corpus, 28
cunctanter, 20

defigo, 26, 28
defixio, 26, 28, 33
detestabilior, 20
devotus, 28

goetia, 20, 78

herba, 28

iecur, 28

langueo, 28

magia, 20, 78
miseror, 28

noceo, 28
nomen, 28

poeniceus, 28
pudibundus, 20

purgatio, 20

rapito, 46

sagave, 28

Thessalia, 28
theurgia, 20

veneno, 28

www.ingramcontent.com/pod-product-compliance
Lightning Source LLC
Chambersburg PA
CBHW020357170426
43200CB00005B/204